**Ben Markus**

**New Jersey Exile**

Ben Markus

# New Jersey Exile

## A music auto-biography (and much much more)

JustFiction Edition

**Impressum/Imprint (nur für Deutschland/only for Germany)**
Bibliografische Information der Deutschen Nationalbibliothek: Die Deutsche Nationalbibliothek verzeichnet diese Publikation in der Deutschen Nationalbibliografie; detaillierte bibliografische Daten sind im Internet über http://dnb.d-nb.de abrufbar.

Alle in diesem Buch genannten Marken und Produktnamen unterliegen warenzeichen-, marken- oder patentrechtlichem Schutz bzw. sind Warenzeichen oder eingetragene Warenzeichen der jeweiligen Inhaber. Die Wiedergabe von Marken, Produktnamen, Gebrauchsnamen, Handelsnamen, Warenbezeichnungen u.s.w. in diesem Werk berechtigt auch ohne besondere Kennzeichnung nicht zu der Annahme, dass solche Namen im Sinne der Warenzeichen- und Markenschutzgesetzgebung als frei zu betrachten wären und daher von jedermann benutzt werden dürften.

Coverbild: www.ingimage.com

Verlag: JustFiction! Edition ist ein Imprint der
LAP LAMBERT Academic Publishing GmbH & Co. KG
Heinrich-Böcking-Str. 6-8, 66121 Saarbrücken, Deutschland
Telefon +49 681 37 20 310, Telefax +49 681 37 20 310-9
Email: info@justfiction-edition.com

Herstellung in Deutschland:
Schaltungsdienst Lange o.H.G., Berlin
Books on Demand GmbH, Norderstedt
Reha GmbH, Saarbrücken
Amazon Distribution GmbH, Leipzig
ISBN: 978-3-8454-4587-8

**Imprint (only for USA, GB)**
Bibliographic information published by the Deutsche Nationalbibliothek: The Deutsche Nationalbibliothek lists this publication in the Deutsche Nationalbibliografie; detailed bibliographic data are available in the Internet at http://dnb.d-nb.de.

Any brand names and product names mentioned in this book are subject to trademark, brand or patent protection and are trademarks or registered trademarks of their respective holders. The use of brand names, product names, common names, trade names, product descriptions etc. even without a particular marking in this works is in no way to be construed to mean that such names may be regarded as unrestricted in respect of trademark and brand protection legislation and could thus be used by anyone.

Cover image: www.ingimage.com

Publisher: JustFiction! Edition
is an imprint of the publishing house
LAP LAMBERT Academic Publishing GmbH & Co. KG
Heinrich-Böcking-Str. 6-8, 66121 Saarbrücken, Germany
Phone +49 681 37 20 310, Fax +49 681 37 20 310-9
Email: info@justfiction-edition.com

Printed in the U.S.A.
Printed in the U.K. by (see last page)
ISBN: 978-3-8454-4587-8

# NEW JERSEY EXILE
## Chapter 1

I was trying to find something BIG to wear from my very limited wardrobe of clothes, Hell I was nervous! Glam Rock was still a few years away but I simply had to look great!

Leather jacket?...no, didn't have one smart enough...frilly shirt?....Christ no! So I borrowed my big brothers winkle pickers, (I say borrowed, more like took them out of the bin) padded out the worn sole with cardboard and thought....denim!......yes!!! 'Status Quo' were still in their Hippy phase with the single 'Black Veils of Melancholy' currently in the charts... At least I thought that I looked unique but I was probably the only one that did!

Later that night I took to the stage to play at a 'local dance' in the quiet Bedfordshire village of Shillington. It was a pleasant summer evening in 1968 and four other embryo musicians joined me in this early bid for a musical career. Our band was called - 'No Entry'. I had made a point of purposefully hanging my electric guitar in a haphazard fashion around my neck. (Spent hours in front of a mirror at home trying to 'Look Cool'.) We thought we were a Prog Rock type of line up but it sounded more like Punk! The lyrics (mostly original material from Madam Hayday) were very anti establishment, the instrumentation was pure over-driven guitar, bass and drums. We were playing through old VOX AC 30 amplifiers screwed for all they were worth, right up to the point there was nothing but an overdrive sound coming out of them. (These were borrowed so we didn't pay too much attention as to whether or not we were damaging them!) I was still to reach my 13th birthday, so technically not even a teenager! but as I climbed the steps up to the stage, I felt like a million dollars!!

*SEX AND DRUGS AND ROCK AND ROLL!*
*(SEX CAME VIA OLD COPIES OF PLAYBOY, DRUGS WERE ANADINS NEEDED FOR THE LOUD NOISE..........THE ROCK AND ROLL WAS REAL THOUGH!)*

Born in New York in the late fifties, my introduction to popular music came courtesy of Dion and the Belmonts thanks to my older brother. He was nearly 10 yrs older than me and into the US type of do-wop bands, the biggest of these being the FOUR SEASONS but many long dead names made up the 'Charts' in the East Coast US sound.

And then I heard 'Because they're young' by Duane Eddy, even before my first day at Kindergarten I knew that was cool. The twangy Gretch sounded like a full-blown Hollywood Production, strings with a sadness that could melt a young boy and I knew from that point I had to be a part of this. I would simply have to get an electric guitar, trouble was I'd still not yet reached six!

In the early 1960's my parents decided to move to England, they'd been back and forth in their minds and had discussed possible destinations, New Zealand, California as well as Europe. My mother had been born in Lancashire and had met my father in the early 1940's. They were both Air-force personal, my father for the US 8th Air-force, my mother with the WRAF and both rose to the rank of senior N.C.O. As the war ended my mother accompanied my father back to the New York/New Jersey area as my father had family throughout the two states whereas my mother had been orphaned since 12 and was more or less passed from Aunt to Aunt. So she had joined the forces and made that her family.

After the war my father continued in Aircraft Mechanics until he made the decision to change to cars and spent his working hours with the massive GM Corp, Pontiac the company he worked for with Vauxhall Motors always a possibility for work should England be their final destination.

My parents had been talking a lot about moving, still very young I wasn't even sure what the conversations were about, I kept hearing 'Europe' in their conversations but I didn't really know what Europe was! I knew a lot about England though, my mother talked about it all the time in the hot New York summers. She longed to be back in the country of her birth, I think the USA, the eastern seaboard at any rate, was too fast, too big and too bold for her. We were then in a suburb of Newark NJ called Bloomfield but it still felt like a City, or at least a piece of one. The schools were big, the cars were big, everything was big and I loved every bit of it.

We had Burgers, Pizza's, 24-hr television with about 10 channels, baseball, a very modern President, 'John Fitzgerald Kennedy', who somehow managed to make everyone feel that the country and the whole world was on track for something really special.

So in the middle of this 'Paradise' the Markus family found itself getting on an ocean liner moored in New York Harbour in the early sixties, doing the Pilgrims trip in reverse. Saying goodbye to its (children's at any rate) heritage, its friends and up until that point...its life.

There were a few photos taken of the day but most of our faces were sullen, one could even say miserable. Still only seven years old, I was just looking forward to the sea journey still quite oblivious to how big a change we were all about to experience.

*BACK TO THE OLD WORLD.*

We landed in Southampton 5 days later after a brief stop in LeHarve, it was raining!....My father had elected to bring a newish top of the range Pontiac sedan with us rather than be faced with buying a car in England. As we waited around the Southampton Dock for the Pontiac to be unloaded a steam train was pulling off the dock, the sound was deafening but the sight was awesome as masses of steam bellowed from the engine. I'd only seen them in films, the NY/NJ trains had all been diesel or electric....It was raining! The air felt different, everything felt different. Finally our car was unloaded and we climbed in to begin the final leg of the journey. We drove to a hotel somewhere between Southampton and London....It was raining!! The towns looked like...well....all I can remember was thinking how wooden the country looked, even the cars looked wooden. (After living with late fifties and early sixties Chevrolets, Buicks and Cadillacs, believe me, an Austin A35 looked wooden!!)

Over the next two days we made our way to Bedfordshire and to the home of one of my mothers aunts. Auntie Lillian was just as my mother described her....English! (Apart from having a German VW!!, I wonder if she ever knew that was in part designed by Adolf Hitler!) The pleasantries lasted a few hours and we were taken to yet another Hotel in the north of Bedfordshire......It was raining!!!! Even at seven I could see a pattern emerging here! It was always bloody raining!!

*SETTLING IN.*

Over the coming months we settled into a mid Bedfordshire home in a mid Bedfordshire village. The locals thought we were weird! Well, we were! We'd lived in the World's Night Spot. I can still clearly remember one night in New York, my mother was in hospital, (fairly serious but she fully recovered) I was left with Rodney and Christine in a sort of coffee bar and given a hamburger to keep me quiet. There was a jukebox in the corner of the place blaring out DooWop while across the road there stood a giant (and I mean about 150' high) soft drink bottle filled with water, it was an advert for I think, Pepsi. But this display was massive, fully lit from the inside and a huge spectacle that dominated the New York skyline in this area of the city. I just sat eating my hamburger and thought "I love living here" even at that young age I felt plugged into the World, I felt this was where it was all happening. The culture change of emigrating to Britain was tremendous and I don't think any of us fully got over it, more so my brother and sister as they were considerably older than me. I had wanted to be a pro baseball player, that was one dream I couldn't see being fulfilled in Bedfordshire!

We were now in Ruraldom where cows roamed the streets!! (well they sometimes did!) and the local pastime was a Sport, (and I use the word very very loosely) the locals called 'Beer Flunking'. Half a dozen men in white smocks standing in a circle, holding hands dancing around in one direction while another man stood in the centre with a stick, onto which was mounted a beer soaked rag. He danced around in the opposite direction to the rest and threw the rag at one of the circle. Whoever he hit then had to drink a huge pitcher of beer, if the man in the middle missed, he had to drink it.....You guessed it......everyone got very drunk very quickly. This certainly was not the World Series at Yankee Stadium!!

*THE COMING!*

The music was, I have to admit.....drab! It was still raining!..... I always thought Cliff Richard was trying to be like the US artists but he just never did it for me. I know a lot like him but I couldn't summon up any enthusiasm. There were other artists in a similar vein, Lonnie Donnegan etc but no Presley.....We all know now there would never be another Presley.......But the next best thing was about to hit the World!!

Rushing home from school on a Rainy day to grab the one hour of television allowed to English children it happened like a bolt out of the Blue and just like the Duane Eddy moment! Four men with long dark hair (they looked like men to me, I was still an ankle biter!) three guitars and drums, playing what I can only describe as the most way out sound I'd ever heard before or since. Looking back now it doesn't seem too different from the Rock and Roll/ Soul sound that came from the US but it was put over somehow differently, probably the equal power of the vocal from John Winston Lennon and Sir Paul McCartney. The guitar playing of George Harrison was quite something too and should never be overlooked by anyone. The four of them looked like they belonged together, looked like they'd always been together and looked like they were going to take over the World together. I sat mesmerised, it didn't take long for me to become a disciple. My big sister wrote the following into one of the current Girl magazines/papers. "My little brother Benji likes the Beatles so much....he combs his eyebrows down to make his hair look longer", the letter was published......It was true.....I did comb my eyebrows.....it just didn't seem to have the right effect!!

For the life of me I don't know how or why....... but it suddenly seemed to have stopped raining!!!

Chapter 2.

These were The 'Beatle' days when contemporary music was once again turned on its head but this time from the English side of the Atlantic Ocean. The first phase of the 'music' revolution had occurred in the USA in and around 1955. Elvis had not been the only soldier, Jerry Lee Lewis, Fats Domino, Chuck Berry to name but a few. Whether the US Government had, as some people have claimed, had anything to do with these early Rock pioneers fading away, if only for a few years, getting called up, being jailed - is anyone's guess. But it was by all accounts, getting a bit stale over there. The clean-cut singers such as 'Fabian', 'Ricky Nelson' and 'Bobby Vee' were now ruling the roost. Christ! popular music needed the 'Beatles' and no one would be disappointed.

The Beatles headed what is now commonly termed the British invasion of the USA. The Beatles were on the top of the pyramid followed closely by; 'The Rolling Stones', 'The Hollies' and 'The Kinks'. For me the ' Stones' were always the 'Bad boys' and I loved them nearly as much but I never thought they had the song-writing skills or the finesse in the recording studio that the Beatles seemed to have. Maybe that was due to George Martin, maybe it wasn't but the English music scene was bursting with talent and for the first time I felt glad my parents had emigrated.

Still too young to play I began listening to the 'Pirate' radio stations, 'Caroline' was my favourite but 'Radio London' was also worth a listen and at night you could tune into 'Radio Luxembourg'. The reception was scratchy, the radios were awful but there were so many ways to listen to what was around. I often copied my heroes, mimicking guitarists with the aid of a fishing rod that had been given to me for a Christmas present, along with an imaginary mic stand in front of me I would play 'Air guitar' long before the album came out. For a visual 'fix' there was always a weekly injection of 'Top of the Pops' to keep everyone interested in who and what was happening.

It was when I was 11yrs old, just on the verge of going to secondary school when my brother came home from his work as a mechanic with a new toy for himself, this toy however would change my life forever!

It was a six string solid bodied electric guitar called a 'Starway', it had a deep brown sunburst finish with 2 pick-ups (guitar microphones). In addition to this it sported a headstock similar in shape to a Fender Stratocaster, coupled to a rosewood fret board this all helped to make the guitar quite stunning to look at. Rodney had done a deal with a workmate, probably for fixing a car I knew I had to have a go when he wasn't looking, even getting close to it made my pulse race.

Luckily the set up of the instrument was not too bad. Many times over the years I've heard of youngsters buying or being bought a guitar, their mother or father would then say to me - "He just won't play it" Then I would try the instrument myself only to discover you'd need hands with the power of a gorilla to push the strings down to the fret board by which time it would be cutting your fingers to Hell!.

But the 'Starway' was quite forgiving and even easy to play. My brother practised whilst listening to 'Shadows' records while trying to pick out the melodies. When he was at work I crept into his bedroom and did the same, it wasn't long before I started to overtake him. I was even beginning to pick out rudimentary chords, mostly basic fifths with a few open C's and G's. One night totally immersed in my playing, I failed to notice him coming up the stairs. Catching me unawares he'd been listening outside the door, Rodney came into the room. I'd been playing 'Wonderful Land' by the Shadows, "you might as well keep it" he said sullenly. I thought I was in trouble but a few weeks later Rodney had bought me a brand new 'Vox Traveller' amplifier to go with the guitar, at the same time putting himself into debt with a hire purchase company for it, I was on my way thanks to John Rodney Markus!!

I was in the first year of secondary school the music on a national footing was taking on a new Progressive twist, bands like ' Spooky Tooth', 'The Nice', ' Circus' and 'Jethro Tull' were all very strong. 'Cream' were the most famous of these bands, Eric Clapton rising to the rank of God if you looked at some of the posters on street corners!. He played like no one else at that time. My personal favourite was Peter Green from 'Fleetwood Mac' but Mr Clapton set the pace and the ball rolling.

This new way of soloing or 'free playing' was totally new to the 'Pop' Bands as these early 'Axemen' made up solo's out of thin air thus returning to a footing more akin to jazz in style and mentality. I just thought it was wild, I've since heard Jack Bruce telling an interviewer "Ginger and I thought we were a Jazz Band....we just never told Eric!" I love that phrase and with hindsight it made sense.

Attempting to seek out others who played I found a group in nearby Barton, Rodney knew of this young Band and suggested I go down and meet them which I did. I stood in a garden shed in Dane Rd Barton while this 4 piece played very dodgy Rock, they were using home made guitars with 3 strings tuned to a root, a 5$^{th}$ and an octave and just 'barred' the 3 strings across. This made a decent amount of noise and it was in tune. The band was at that time; Geoff Howlett, (whose father made the guitars) Phil Rowlands and Pete Smith, with Madam Hayday (I never knew what his real name was) on vocals, all these lads came from Barton. Geoff had a spare guitar (handmade of course) which he offered to me, I picked it up and played along, keeping up was fairly easy as it was just laying the fingers across a fret. At the end of the first rehearsal I was asked to join and with one other member Bob Virgin, we went out as 'No Entry'. I'm proud to say I never altered the tuning on the 'Starway' electing to at least try and play it properly. I always kept 6 strings and always played the lead on the instrumental numbers. These included;

'Walk Dont Run' by 'The Ventures', 'Rinky Dink' by Lord knows who and 'Wipe Out'. I started to notice just how the girls seemed to be affected by music!!! Wow this is great, in a Band at 12 yrs old and getting female attention!!

The Band carried on with this line up throughout the next year, school gigs, Village hall gigs, party gigs. £5-6 per night was the fee, it might sound a pittance now but it wasn't then. Getting £1 each was great, a single was around 25p each, an album £2, AND my apprenticeship was being served. A lot of the time we were playing at least 1 and sometimes 2 gigs a week, playing mostly original material. A local guitarist Peter Payne became interested and started teaching the band as a whole but I'd started getting itchy feet. I think one or two of my comrades were just trying to play for the girls in the crowds but I was starting to realise I wanted something different. The female attention was great...But I wanted much more.

I started listening very carefully to production techniques on the records of my icons, how they sometimes used overdrive sounds or sometimes a clean sound. Jimmy Page and Led Zeppelin were for me the Pinnacle in this field, Led Zeppelin II still stands today as one of my favourite all time albums.

I started to learn just how versatile a guitar could be on a production footing, LZII was awesome in the late sixties when it appeared and equals the 'best' that was around at that time.

I also realised just how good an electric guitar could feel in your hands after the guitarist in a local semi-pro band, 'UNIT 6' let me play his 'Gibson SG Custom'. It was like nothing I'd played before, the feel of the neck, the way you could run your fingers across the fret-board, It felt like another world in comparison to the 'Starway'

I asked him how much if he were to sell the 'SG'? £50 was the reply....where on earth can I get 50 quid from??? But I knew I would somehow, although it would still be a few years before I was in that bracket of instrument.

'No Entry' slowly came to an end, a variety of reasons, no single incident, it just slowly petered out. Geoff Howlett and I formed another 3 piece. By now I thought my soloing had reached a stage to make it a feature of the Band. Neil Mattocks joined us on drums and we did another year or so with this modified line up. Geoff did a lot of the vocals, he was never the strongest voice but he managed pretty well. Geoff and Neil were more in tune with my frame of mind as to where we wanted to go with music, we would often discuss trying to record properly but we were still fairly ignorant of studios.

*TERRY WHITE'S – LUTON LEGEND.*

I'd also begun playing with a smallish line up in SILSOE, just hanging out with the gang at first but we got together on a regular basis in the village hall and more or less jammed all night. Myself, John Nixon from school on bass, his friend Jeremy Wilkinson on guitar and 'Boot' Brazier on drums was the line up. We only ever practised but it was more the style of music I wanted to be playing. Bands like 'Steamhammer', 'Chicago' (the early 'heavy' line up) 'King Crimson' and Fleetwood Mac were now on top of the pile in this neck of the woods at any rate.

John Nixon was probably my best friend at this stage, one of his friends was Simon Wood. Not a player himself, Simon had two elder brothers, Richard and Chris who were full blown hippies and very into the 'Progressive' music scene. John, Simon and I would more often than not, end up in a room in Simon's house that his brothers had decked out in posters and a music system, archaic by today'ss standards but huge by the usual phonogram stds in most peoples houses. Basically a small turntable hooked up to a 100w bass guitar amplifier....Potent! (It's a wonder Mother and Father Wood didn't have a breakdown due to the level of noise we played everything at but they were very accommodating to the numbers of teenagers in their lovely old house.)

9

The three brothers combined music taste was impeccable. I was introduced to music NO ONE I knew of in my age group was listening to; Pink Floyd, Dr John, Frank Zappa, Captain Beefheart, Blind Faith, Mel Collin's Circus, John Hiseman's Coliseum, The Doors and a host of lesser known Artists who all produced albums to a very high standard thus giving me a glimpse into a much bigger universe. While the Silsoe band never amounted to much in the 'Live playing' stakes, we did make regular trips to a Luton Music shop called 'Terry White's'.

I'd never met Terry White, he'd died a short time before, his widow then took over the reigns and employed a manager who really only seemed interested in getting friends and muso's around to jam with. The Jam sessions were without doubt FANTASTIC! The standard of musicianship way beyond any band I had seen or played with up until that point and therefore a brilliant training ground for me.

I learned more in this phase than all the previous musical environments put together. Watching the various guitarists who were in a different league to me, jamming with them when they let me, which I have to admit they often did. They were all to a man, good to me, I was much younger at 14 – 15 and they were all 18 and above but they let me hang around with them...And I learned! My greatest teacher at this time was 'Milky', Alan Mickleborough was a very jovial individual, a shade more Charismatic than the rest, his guitar technique was brilliant. A Blues-man through and through, he made a guitar sound like it was joined to his hip. How he managed that at such an early age was beyond me. He'd give me tips on how to bend notes, vibrato and then when we all got kicked out of 'Terry White's' because the owner had popped in unannounced, I would follow them up to the café and Milky usually ended up buying me a bacon sandwich.

I'm still great friends with 'Milky' but we had lost touch for 20 yrs. A couple of years ago I asked a local paper on the back of a review for a new album to mention if anyone knew the whereabouts of 'Milky'. Sort of a 'Have you seen this man' type article, the paper happily obliged. 'Milky' was receiving calls left right and centre and managed to get my number. We met up and he sometimes plays with 'MARKUS' today when the workload of his own band lets him.

*SCHOOL DAYS*

I never really took to school for a variety of reasons, suffice to say I would be much happier working for a living. It was one of the best days of my life when I left and no longer had to turn up for the painfully slow trip to school.

I had been in the Grammar Stream but I had left with no exams under my belt. I worked at a few places, a transport firm, an electronics firm (where I was the only male working with 30 plus women!) and a couple of weeks on a coal round. Pat Goddard was the boss, he wasn't that bothered with things like laws. I was 15 yrs old and driving a 15 ton coal lorry around Bletchley with Pat sleeping in the passenger seat, I thought this was great, I was driving a lorry!!

That job didn't last long however, for months Pat had been using his lorry without a Commercial vehicle ticket. You can do things like that for a while but the police will pull you over eventually. They did! A motorcycle Policeman gave Pat the usual routine ticket to show the vehicle documents at a police station in five days time, we got back into the vehicle and drove off, Pat was driving now, I sat reading out the items on the list. "It's OK Pat, you've got your driving licence?" Yes was the reply. "You've got Insurance?" Again positive response. "You've got the MOT?" "Ah well no, I umm, haven't got that just yet".... I thought it was time for a change of job anyway!! I did a few things here and there and ended up operating earth-moving machinery in the London Brick works. The pay was excellent. Job satisfaction was non-existent.

On my 16th birthday motorcycles took my attention for a few months at any rate. My BSA 250 filling a portion of my life followed by bigger and bigger bikes, where will it all end?? Yup, in hospital! Only minor injuries though. Keeping bikes until the present day I did calm down a bit and re-focused on music. I was asked by a local Rock and Roll outfit, 'Chris Cole and the Wildcats' to join them on guitar.

*LOCAL HERO.*

Chris Cole was known to everyone in the mid Beds area, (still is today) a full blown Rocker, he was a few years older than me but we got on well. (Everyone got on with Chrissy!). Being in this band also allowed me to amalgamate motorcycles with music.

Chrissy was the nations biggest BSA fan, not just the singles but the company's twins too. One coldish night in autumn the two of us set out on his Gold Flash combo with Swallow sidecar to get some gigs around the Luton/Hitchin area. It was already dark, I was cold before we set off and my leather wasn't in the best condition. At least I had the sidecar that I could duck into. Chrissy threw me his Golden Virginia and cigarette papers. "Keep 'em coming Boy!" Expecting me to roll his cigarettes, light them, and pass them to him throughout the journey.

Its extremely hard to roll cigarettes, light them, and pass them to the driver when your bouncing all over the bloody road at breakneck speeds. (It was 1973, it felt like break neck speeds!!) I dropped more than one, the minute I handed them across and they got into the wind-stream, they were gone in about 30 seconds. "Come on....give us another" I spent the whole journey trying to roll his fags....I felt like his Bitch!

We pulled up at venue after venue and got loads of bookings, every place we stopped someone knew Chrissy. By now we were miles from our home territory but someone would still come up to us with the familiar phrase... "Bloody Chris Cole....how you doin mate?"

Rock and Roll the pure stuff, was never my greatest love, for playing at any rate. I did like to listen to it though, especially to the Chuck Berry material and his style of playing. I'd begun playing the 'Berry' style of 2 note solos while in Chris Cole's Band. I always rated Chuck Berry as a guitarist as much as I rated his Gibson 335 guitar but a lot didn't. Guitarists then thought it was long in the tooth but he was soloing the crowds into a frenzy long before the Axe Men of the 60's and 70's, I still use a piece of that style today.

### REAL GUITARIST!

The Starway was getting to be an embarrassment, it was totally without stature. I was working plus getting gig money so time for a change. A close friend Paul Millard drove me to Bletchley, I'd earmarked a black 1957 Fender Stratocaster after telephoning all the local music shops. The Bucks shop had it up for £150. Paul was horrified I was wasting so much money on something as foolish as a guitar saying more than once "You can buy a bloody good bike for that money!" I handed over the cash and took the Fender home, now I was a 'Real' Guitarist.....in looks at any rate!.

The money was coming in with the Rock and Roll band so I could afford quite luxurious cars, a Pontiac was one of the flashiest followed by a number of Jag's, Ford Zodiacs and...well...anything I fancied really.

Around this time my father died of heart disease, he had smoked a lot and ate the wrong foods. Heart disease was going to be a big problem for the coming generations and a long time before people would start to realise how bad Cholesterol and nicotine was for the cardiopulmonary system.

I'd also auditioned for a Luton Prog Rock Band, this WAS more what I wanted to do. We never got as far as choosing a name but we began rehearsing what for me, was the first really serious band I had been connected with. Strange how you view something, even though I was earning more than most with the Rock and Roll band, I still never perceived it as 'Proper' or took it seriously.

*LOST IN SPACE.*

This line up never seemed to get any songs finished on a production basis. Peter (the leader and singer) seemed to change his mind from one rehearsal to the next on how he wanted things done. His girlfriend sat in the corner passing judgement, rolling very very strange looking cigarettes and acting for want of a better term, spaced out! (I thought at the time it must've been a bad batch of Golden Virginia!!) I spent months with this 4 piece rehearsing Hendrix tracks, Jethro Tull tracks, I just wanted to meet someone who could write songs and begin forming something new but it just wasn't happening. At the end of 3 months we were no nearer to playing in front of an audience than the first day.

I became disillusioned to the point that I was thinking, "This isn't for me". I was 18, doing a job I hated in the local brick yards and feeling very trapped.

I saw an article in the local paper 'JOIN THE FIRE SERVICE' with a very cheesy picture depicting a 'Hero' type on top of a ladder rescuing a Damsel in distress, however it worked!............I applied

Chapter 3.

*QUEEN AND COUNTRY (but no FREDDIE MERCURY!)*

Back in New Jersey we had lived near a Fire Station, my mother occasionally took me there to see the big red engines. The minute you enter a Fire Station the vehicles instantly take over your focus and to this day I can't explain it. There's a power and a mystique about a bay full of Fire Engines, its not the same when they are in a museum. Maybe it's the vibe from the ones that are in service, or as the Brigade call it, 'Used in Anger' but most young boys can feel it. Its compelling, it's a Kind of Magic!

After reading the advert I went along one Saturday morning to The Bedfordshire Fire Service's Brigade Control where one of the control staff gave me the inside story on what it was like to be a Fireman. (We were firemen! Not Fire-fighters, not fire people.....FIREMEN!!!)

Chum Lazenby, one of the control staff gave me an application form, I filled it all in, posted it off and waited. Many exams, physical tests and medical examinations later I was given orders to report to Brigade Training School.

I never thought for a moment it would be hard work, how hard can it be to squirt a hose around for a while!!! My world had been turned upside down yet again. Hose drills started the first day, the instructors broke us in gently by not shouting abuse at us for at least 2 hours! Ladder running drills, hose drills, rescue drills, all done at the double and twice weekly long distance running! I hated long distance running!! I've always hated Long Distance Running!!! Ask anyone who knows me, you know what they'll say? "BEN HATES LONG DISTANCE RUNNING!!!!"

One of these lovely sojourns into the English countryside found me with my face firmly in the mud (it was winter) just wishing I could die peacefully. (God I could do with a Fag!!) Sinking into the mud now covering the front of my body, I was lying face down totally exhausted. Pat Wheeler should've been a counsellor for the nervous. He was a 6'4" Drill instructor and had a physical menace about him that could make Mafia Hit-men cringe. He knelt down beside me and bellowed into my ear, "DON'T JUST LIE THERE MARKUS!!! DO PRESS UPS!!" and he wasn't joking.

Midway through the 12 week course things started getting a teensy bit easier, I was no longer

14

falling asleep in front of the telly at 7pm, I could last until nearly nine o clock before my mother would throw a blanket over me and go to bed herself. My body was getting fitter, fitter than it had ever been before, it felt pretty good. Of the 12 recruits that had begun the course nine were now left, I was very proud to be one of the nine. My mother seemed to be too, she confided in me at the Brigade 'Pass Out' day that she never thought I'd make it through the twelve weeks....I confided back....."You know what?...neither did I!!"

I survived basic training and received my posting to Luton Fire Station, Studley Rd. It was a busy station receiving at its peak 3,300 calls per year. My family life had not been what I would call a family life, my father had died 2 yrs before. Many factors that do not need airing here had been at work but suffice to say I had been a bit lost on the family front.....I now had my family. Luton White Watch had its paternal figures, its maternal figures (sorry Mac, but you've always been like a 'Mum' to me!) and my siblings in my fellow rookies. There were arguments, there were disagreements, there was a lot of laughter and friendships made that continue to this day. The Fire Service became my home and I loved it.

Because I was motivated, I undertook every exam and qualification I could but I still cherished above all else, driving the Big Red Fire Engines. (The Fire Brigade hates anyone calling them Fire Engines, they call them Appliances or Pumps...I still call them Fire Engines....at least when no one from the Fire Service is around!!) I passed my Brigade driving test first time and was 'On the Run' as a driver before my 23rd birthday. The pumps in the main had very big powerful engines, they had to so they could meet the Home Office laid down figures for speed and acceleration. My favourite was Fleet 79, a 1973 Dennis Water Tender Ladder code named '313' (based on its radio call sign). Every 'first' that occurred for me, first fire, first drive to a fire, first BA (breathing apparatus) job seemed to happen when I was on Fleet 79.

Jack Jackson was usually around too, he was the officer on the pump for my first drive, he was driving the pump on my first shout, he had more or less adopted me. (And still comes to 'Gigs to this day!)

One of these Dennises had a crash gearbox. Driving Jacko down the road to a non fire destination, I crunched the gearbox. Jack had his marlin spike out of its holster threatening to crack my knuckles if I crunched the box. The minute the gears crunched I quickly let the gear stick go.....CLANG went the marlin spike as it hit the gear stick. "Nyaaaaa, you missed me Jack" I gloated.....The minute I changed gear again. THWACK! He got me..

(I could write reams and reams about the Fire Service, in fact I did in 1988. The manuscript went to Buchan & Enright where Dominique Enright became very interested and told me how to do a re-write of the script. Just as it looked like it might get published...well it just didn't happen. (I think the company was going through some financial troubles in common with the rest of the World!)

There were deaths, multiple deaths, suicides in fires and arson attempts by businessmen trying to get insurance money. Children whose parents failed to get them out from horrendous fire situations, (of which we also failed). Watching a mother come apart at the seams as you tell her that her little girl had died is not something I want to go into in great detail here and now other than to say I saw horrific sights. I had the great days when we just made it into a slum type property in the nick of time, grabbed the children out from under their beds where they'd been hiding, made the escape down the staircase and collapsed into a heap outside, retching your guts up into the gutter due to the amount of smoke you'd inhaled. Then....lighting up a fag coz you needed it badly! (This was a Great day!!) The Fire Service taught me a huge amount about life. I think it helped me to be a better father than I might have been had I not experienced 9 yrs on a busy fire station. I know it made me grow as a person and see life in a different light. I would not under any circumstance have changed those 9 yrs but neither would I long for them again.

*What's the name of that f\*\*\*ing Indian?*

During those Fire Service years I met Sharon, married her and we had 4 wonderful children. (I know that's a teensy bit of condensing but if you want to read about 'relationships' bloody well go read 'Bridget Jones's Diary', this is about music!!!) Sadly we separated 20 yrs after marrying but to this day we are still good friends.

We did get one different holiday though. Sharon wanted to go parachuting!! When I agreed it seemed a very long way off, I sometimes have trouble seeing that far into the future so I agreed to join her. Five months later I was driving to Leominster for a week long course at the Hereford Parachute Club and wondering how the hell I could get out of this. I couldn't chicken out with my wife doing a jump, maybe I can twist my leg as I get out of the car!! But then I thought...she'll back out before the decent!! We did the basic days training, we were there for the whole week though I hoped it would rain all week! (see UK Weather trends Chapter One.....never when you bloody need it though). The next day I had the 32' parachute pack on my back as I climbed into the old air-plane. Static line operated parachutes were the type ALL first timers used, i.e. you just fall out of the air-plane, you didn't have to pull anything or operate anything. Static line parachutes are incredibly reliable.

Sharon was on the first plane load, I was on the second. I watched her plane take off and gain height, at around 2,500 ft all of her plane load one by one came out the door, Sharon included! Shit....I'm gonna have to do it now! My plane came around to pick up the load I was part of. The take off was a very new experience, hang on a minute!! I'VE NEVER FLOWN BEFORE!! I hadn't realised until we were barrelling down the runway in the old Cessna 206 that flying was also going to be a 'first' for me today. These types of planes are never what you'd call quiet inside, removing the doors doesn't exactly help this situation, all that filled the world was noise. We approached the DZ run, 'Kip' Kibblewhite hung his head out of the door looking for the drop point. (The distance away from the target circle on the ground that takes into account wind drift, technically speaking you'll hit the bulls-eye.....Although hit might not be the best word to use here!) Kip motioned for me to take up position in the doorway, I dangled my legs out of the door, he shouted to the pilot. "Five left, five left, CUT!" The pilot cut the engine. "GOOOOOOOO!" I'm not sure if I jumped on my own or he pushed me but I was dropping like a stone, I know my heart rate must've been in the 200's. Then Plop, the canopy opened softly and I was drifting down. God that old army type canopy looked good. Then just behind I heard a voice where I really wasn't expecting one, "You Ugly Bastard, what're you doing?" Kip had followed me out the door as I was the last of that particular load and we descended the 2,000 feet together.

Jesus Christ! That was great!! 7 more descents in the week and I was hooked. I started coming back on my days off from the Fire Station and eventually got a qualification as a manifester and packer with the possibility of working with KIP and his mate Dave Howerski. They both told me they'd teach me everything they knew about skydiving. (They were however very drunk at the time and I was driving them home!)

Many parachuting buffs will know that Paul 'Kip' Kibblewhite died in the German accident in the early 1980's. He had been with 50 other parachutists on a 'Display'. An air-force helicopter's blades sheared off at a low height causing the aircraft to crash. The Daily Mail carried a photo of the chopper seconds before it hit the ground, one parachutist managed to get out of the door but he was too low for his canopy to open. I wondered if it might've been Kip? I thought again, no, he

17

would've been trying to get the others out first....

Bands took a back seat for those Fire Service years, I still played occasionally with Chrissy, time permitting from the busy shift pattern. In addition I also half-heartedly put together a couple of Bands but nothing ever came from them. I thought I would live out my working life as a Fireman, probably at Luton Fire Station. But as life does, it throws us what looks like a curve....but we're occasionally still able to hit it out of the Ballpark!! (God I love baseball terms!)

*IT WAS A DARK AND STORMY NIGHT!*

Things had been steady, maybe too steady if that's possible. My life had never been steady, well I didn't think so. I hadn't been feeling great, a few headaches that never seemed to go away. As we do, I just thought, oh well, a couple of headaches but they always seemed to be there, many's the time on waking I felt almost like I was wrapped in cling film and everything was a bit surreal and dream like. Then one morning I woke with Sharon looking horrified at me, the bed was covered in blood! I felt like Crap with a capital 'C' an 'R' and probably the 'A' and 'P' too!

At approx five in the morning I had disturbed Sharon while she slept, she wasn't sure what was happening but I was in physical trouble. My whole body had apparently gone into a spasm and every single muscle had tensed. I had been lying on my side with my right hand resting on top of my left bicep. When the spasm occurred, my hand clenched tightly and my four fingers of my right hand pierced the left bicep. The wound was significant and to this day I still have 4 scars in my left bicep where the finger nails went into it. She'd tried in vain to wake me then called the doctor, at which point I noticed him sitting on the other side of the bed. "What the Hells going on?" was about all I could say. He didn't know, I surely didn't know. I became frightened.

Signed off sick from the Service, the wounds in my arm were enough for a sick-note, they did a few tests over the next month at the local hospital as an Out Patient. Heart ECG, brain EEG all seemed ok. Dr Morgan-Hughes resident Neurologist at Bedford South Wing and all round Good guy (He was one of the nicest doctors I ever met!) told me not to worry about the incident, just go about life as normal and he would sign me fit to go back on duty. Before the wounds could heal properly it happened again. I know this won't sound too intelligent for anyone reading but I wanted to stay a Fireman and I knew a problem of this nature would soon end that, so I told Sharon not to call anyone if another seizure occurred.

18

This time I was completely out from five in the morning until dinnertime. Sharon was obviously very scared so she called the doctor, rightly so. He arrived soon after at about 2 pm and examined me, gave me an injection, of what I don't know, and I started coming around.

I can still remember what he said as he left. "I'll give the National Hospital for Nervous Disease a call, it's probably just an embolism or something like that!"

Ohh thanks Doc....for a minute I was worried!! Thanks for making me feel better!!

The National (as it was then known) called within the hour, telling me I had to be there for 9 am the following morning. I was, I have to admit, becoming more scared by the hour. Not the type of scared I'd experienced in the Fire Service, you always somehow knew whatever situation you found yourself in, somehow you'd get out of it, or your colleagues would get you out of it. This was different.

We both arrived at the central London hospital in Queen Square at the appointed time. Sharon was now heavily pregnant with our first child, this wasn't a great time for this to be happening! (Mind you, I can never think of a good time for something like this to happen but you know what I mean!) I knew I was staying in, but somewhere in the back of my mind I wasn't really sure I would get to come out again. I felt like a frightened little boy. As before when I've been in hospital (quite a few times really, 3 motorcycle accidents, a couple of days here and there from Fire Service injuries) ALL the staff were fantastic. The nurses, the doctors. I couldn't have wished for better treatment and  much more importantly, they gave me sympathy but not in a wussy way. Always in a positive manner. Sharon could not get in to London much, one nurse who's name I forget but can still see her face very clearly, sat up with me on more than one night and just talked with me. I don't know if I was more scared of losing my life or my career, it see-sawed between the two.

I was on the Morgan ward with 6 other men all with similar problems or muscle wasting diseases. Again names don't spring sharply to mind but I can remember every single face. One name not consigned to the re-cycle bin was Eric. He was in his forties and had one of the muscle wasting diseases, his diagnosis wasn't good. In fact there was no future and it was going to be slow humiliating death. He had a very sharp mind and the 6 of us formed a poker school, or was it crib? it's been a while.  We all talked on a real level that we just couldn't manage with our spouses and friends. They didn't know, couldn't know what we were going through. But we could share it here with each other on a painfully honest level.  One night when we'd nearly smoked ourselves to death. (I really didn't know I could smoke 30 fags in an evening....but I did!)  Eric was saying, "She (meaning his wife) just talks about me now, in front of me, like I'm some kind of fucking moron who can't hear or understand, so I just dribble on command now!" (It was in the 3$^{rd}$ week of my stay and looking like I was not suffering from anything that would be fatal.)  We were split 50 50 those of us that were going to live or die. Eric leaned over "You'll be going home Ben....you do something with your life....You do it for us!"  I have never told anyone of this and it hurts to remember it... even today.

*REPRIEVE.*

My tests were all in. I had an area of scar tissue damage in an area of my brain. This gave the impression on the CT brain scans of the day of a tumour. BUT...It wasn't growing and it wasn't anything that would grow.

I was by now on quite a few drugs to deal with the seizures but as Dr Morgan-Hughes told me. "The affected area will naturally be 'by-passed' by the surrounding neural pathways. It was also deemed to have been from a very heavy blow to the head.

Four months earlier I had been responding to a Fire call on the station, running to the pump I jumped over a chair and went head-first into a support beam.  I've had a few bumps and collisions over the years but this was the only time I was ever knocked out completely. This was deemed to be the offending injury. At the time of the blow I was kept  in the Luton and Dunstable hospital over night but the scar tissue damage was not found, just concussion. But, and this was the big blow, I had to leave the Fire Service due to the nature of the injury. If I should receive another blow to the head, it could prove fatal, not only could, but likely.
I lost my driving licence for a short time but that would be restored if things went ok with seizures, which they did. But losing your Job AND your driving licence really makes you feel you're just about worthless!  So.....What the Hell do I do now???

20

Chapter 4.

I previously mentioned how 'live' playing had taken a bit of a back seat during my Fire Service time but I'd not finished with music by any means. I became very interested in recording and I had bought a second hand sound on sound reel to reel tape recorder. I could do all the over dubs myself and build up recordings. I even did the drums on these early rough recordings. Initially it was just great fun to do covers but after a month or two, this became a bit boring, so I started writing songs seriously. Judging by the feedback from those around me.....I was good at it.

The early stuff was immature but I grew. It became more and more easy to write songs. Lyrics were usually of a Bluesy nature, but that went with the style of guitarist I was anyway. I sent some of those early home recordings to a number of record labels. (God I hope these have all been placed in rubbish bins and none survive!!) Every time I returned home from a shift, I would check the street to see if a limo was waiting for me......I didn't know!.....It could've happened. Everyone at the start of this type of endeavour thinks to themselves that they are the only one's doing music, or writing a book. It doesn't enter into your thought process there are millions who have been this way before.

So now I was without a career and had very little direction in my life. To her credit, Sharon suggested I get a really decent guitar. I'd been using copies for a while, selling my last decent guitar in order to buy a house. The last of these was a Rickenbacker, one of the rare ones. A 6 string WITH the sought after 'F'holes in the body, as opposed to the cutaway slits, a deep metallic red body being its highlight.

Sharon sensed I needed something to keep going. I found a nice used Fender Telecaster, one from the better years. I never was a big Tele fan but it was the right price and it was a start.

I also realised I was growing out of the abilities the Reel to Reel could offer and needed a pro recording studio if I was to progress with recorded music. A friend from school was in a band that was rising above the usual standard and had a good name for their 'Live Show' which included 'Fire Breathing!!' I contacted Steve Woodward's mother, she told 'Woody' and he called me a few nights later. We were going to meet up, to chat mainly. I had not seen him for 10 years or more.

Sharon gave birth to Melanie Rose Markus, weighing in at 6lbs exactly on Sunday May 16th 1982 at

21

11.53 hrs. She was the bonniest little girl I had ever seen and we took to each other straight away.

I had, as many men may empathise, worried about how I would face up to this new responsibility, would I want to run away? would I behave in a way that was immature? On that bright sunny Sunday I could feel a transformation within myself as I suddenly realised what it truly meant to selflessly love another being. That feeling would return a total of four times in the coming decades.

Steve and his wife Sue came around about this time in May. Steve and I chatted at length about the music industry, recording, you name it, it came up. He was in a local heavy metal band called 'Tobruk' they were signed to 'Neat Records' in Newcastle with interest from the massive EMI Record label. Then he was on bass but his forte was a guitarist. He readily agreed to help me to do some recordings of my songs. I'd booked 'Spaceward studios in Cambridge, a really nice 24track analogue studio using a 'Studer' with a lovely big desk. The crew there were all very helpful and I looked forward to the 1 day session of 14 hrs. We'd planned to record 3 tracks in the day session, from start to finish, instruments, vocals, mix, everything!

That one day session taught me NEVER to record like that again. We came away with some very good recordings, but it was murder on the mind and body.

Joe Bull was my first engineer on that day. We recorded 3 songs, 'Recant', 'When you're gone and 'Life is Cruel'.
Steve's friend and 'Tobruk' colleague Alan Valance offered to do the drumming. Steve helped an enormous amount with the workload of the day. I was still a virgin in this professional atmosphere. I never initially wanted to do the vocals, I just couldn't find anyone else to perform the songs, who would also be cheap enough. My voice was ok but never how I wanted it to be

We turned up at around 10 o clock in the morning to the converted old school house. It looked a pretty cool building, just the type of place where you would expect 'Rock' to be born. The basic tracks were laid down on all 3 songs, guitar, bass and drums. Then we started doing the overdubs, guitar, then lead vocals, then backing vocals finally mixing to a finished state ready for vinyl. I was so new at this and it really was amazing that we completed the 3 tracks to a high standard. This was in the main due to the talents of Steve Woodward and Joe Bull.

During Melanie's early years, Sharon often carried on working while I looked after our baby

22

daughter. So she was there on that first session in her carry-cot with me. Midway through a guitar take, I was playing the solos, I had to stop because her nappy needed changing. I'm in the control room of Spaceward Recording Studios,where the day before Dave Stewart and Barbara Gaskin had completed a new single and I begin changing my daughter's nappy. The look of horror on these hippies faces as I completed the task was a picture. It was like I'd shown them just how truly horrible the Universe could really be!! With this type of background however, its no wonder Melanie grew up being very musical, although I suspect, that's also due to her raw talent!.

I now had 3 tracks to a fully mastered state. Everything in the 80's was passed around by cassette. The horrible devices that never play the same as a master tape but it was all we had. I began sending copies out to the various record labels. EMI, Polydor, Phonogram, CBS, you name it, I'd had a rejection letter from them with the old recordings.....But this had to be different!!! Soon the rejection letters started rolling in!.....Christ don't they know good stuff!!!

*TAKE ME FOR A TRIP UPON....*

I think I'd started growing immune to rejection. Another letter, yea yea, "Dear etc, thank you for thinking of Blahh Blahh blahh, its just not what we want at the moment" Signed Bollocky Bill or whatever. I wonder if people in the big companies know how soul-destroying form letters really are. They can't even take the time to write a bloody letter when we've put in so much effort and money. I still hadn't realised how oversubscribed the record companies truly were.
Then one morning opening up another rejection letter...."SHARON" I shouted. "This one likes it and they want to see me!!!"

John Hewlett at A & M Records in London liked the Spaceward tape and asked me to go down for a meeting! "There has to be a mistake" I said to Sharon. "This must've been for someone else!" Where's my rejection letter They were much easier to deal with!

What the Hell am I going to wear!!! Leather....no.....frilly shirt....Christ no!.....Denim....Ever had the feeling of Deja Vue!!

*THE KINGS ROAD.*

A & M records were in Chelsea. Their biggest act as everyone knew, was the band - 'Police', they had signed some really big artists over the years. The place looked like a Record company should, the receptionists were all Glamour girls and there was an expensive air to the place. For a spell I felt like a big artist. John Hewlett was great. We talked at length, mostly about the direction my music was going. He did ask if I would like to change to a sort of a Punky/New Romantic style. I wasn't really sure what he meant, whether a change of clothing or a change in the musical style? As he took me down to the staff restaurant for a coffee, he showed me a room. It was about 20 ft by 25 with a huge table in the middle, this was swamped with cassettes stacked virtually head height!

"This is how many tapes we get over a short period" John told me and continued. "I pick up a couple on my way home at night and play them in the car...Yours happened to be one I picked up that night. Every month we clear them out and put them in the rubbish." How many possible Beatles or Stones or Whitney Houston's are in those bins? How many Jacksons or Jethro Tulls are consigned to the bin without ever being heard? How many young peoples hearts are broken by the fact no letter had come their way.? Thousands! But maybe the weeding process has to be this tough. It's not just about talent. It's about tenacity, more so than talent. Maybe it shouldn't be, but I think it sorts itself out in the grand order of things. Maybe some get hurt but maybe they'd get hurt more if other scenarios were to become reality? I don't know. I'm a bloody guitarist...not a bloody philosopher!! (Even if I do dress like John Paul Sattra!!!)

I liked John Hewlett, he was a real stand up guy and they were very sparse in an industry that tends to deal in bullshit. We talked for most of the afternoon and he suggested I put 2 of the 3 tracks onto a single and release it myself and see what happens with the radio stations, see if they'd give it any airtime. The idea was a good one, I'd not thought of that. He wanted to see some feedback on me before going any further. If you're reading John, thank you, that meeting turned things for me. I started to believe it could work!.

*A WHOLE NEW WORLD*

I'm not old, mid forties, really not old. (I keep telling myself at this at least once a day) But things have changed drastically in the past 10 or so years with recorded music and even more so with artwork and the way the finished product is achieved. We recorded onto analogue tape machines, we mastered on analogue tape machines. We edited by cutting tape and gluing it back together again. Computerised mixing was something done in the Warp drive of the Starship Enterprise! To make an album, or single it was all copy artwork. That is literally pieces of paper with other pieces of paper stuck to them. Letraset wording carefully placed onto the artwork, then the whole package taken to printers for plate making.

I began to learn just how much work making a record was but I loved every minute of it. I found a company in St Ives Cambridge where the lovely Karen Richardson worked, we got on from the start and she helped me to learn about making records with her pressing company 'Sound Recording Technology'. She was the daughter of one of the directors but she was there on ability pure and simple. She knew how to run things and things ran properly when she ran them.

The first single was a double A side (Well it wasn't really, but people seemed to like what I termed the B side better...so we called it a double A. We had to scratch out the B's and put stickers on them!!) This completed, we gave them out or sent them to all the Radio One Producers and Presenters. Radio one was still the biggest UK station, I think Radio Two today has a bigger audience but Radio One then had about 7 million listeners. We really were just sailing in the wind here. Sharon helped with everything she could. Then early one morning she shouted up, I was still in bed!!

"It's the BBC" she said. I replied "You're going to have to do better than that to get me out of bed at this time!!" Her voice became higher in pitch!

"BEN....COME QUICK". It was Dave Atkey, then producer for Peter Powell.

"We like your single Ben, its going to be on the 5 – 45 Spot next Tuesday"

Thanks I said, still not 100% sure if it was some Fire Service 'Clown' winding me up!

It wasn't a Clown, Fire Service or otherwise. I think I told just about everyone I knew, and then some. My mother had a better radio so we went over to hers for the teatime play and recorded it along with Peter Powell's comments. He liked it a lot, saying there was a lack of 'guitar rock' around in today's play-lists. Melanie was sitting on my knee gurgling as the self penned song played, my mother had been, before her Air-force days, a very good pianist also acquiring a degree with the London College of Music. Quite a feather in the cap for a northern girl but she always classed 'Rock' as Devil music, I think that day she was secretly proud though.

This was the first national play but my first performance on radio was with Nick Barraclough on BBC Radio Cambridge. Having just the cassette tapes, he called and said it would be on his show on a Friday afternoon. It felt wonderful hearing your own songs/recordings played over the airwaves. I just hoped I could keep it going.

Chapter 5.

The BBC gave us 'acceptance' by playing the track 'Life is Cruel' I'd not even thought about distribution. So here we were, having a record played but no one could buy it. I had taken a few around to the Bedford and Luton Record shops, they all readily agreed to take them on a 'Sale or Return' basis but there was so much still to learn. Christ was there still a lot to learn! I'd really cottoned on to the idea of having my own record label though and wanted to pursue this further. I liked the idea of being in charge of it all. I made the time to go around so I could talk with record shop owners in Bedford and Luton and got the low-down on which companies were good and how it all worked. The local press were great, giving me reviews and advice. Mick Sharp, with the Bedfordshire Times as it was once called, gave me a lot of good press in the weekly paper. I was getting more than the local politicians. (I was working harder though)

The next and obvious step was to make an album. Spaceward studios in Cambridge would be good, I wondered if there was anywhere nearer (and maybe a bit cheaper). I looked in the Yellow Pages and found Pace Studios in Milton Keynes. Calling the number a very knowledgeable sound engineer answered, knew exactly what I was after and we hit it off right away.

He was Nigel Pegrum, the drummer with 'Steeleye Span', also of 'Uriah Heep' and 'Gnidrolog'. He owned 'Pace' and knew production well. Pleasantries over we began work on my first album – 'Nocturn Gate'. Alan Valance was a very good drummer but Nigel had told me he could manage it, I still didn't know who he was at this point. He finished a drum 'take' on the first of the newly penned songs, his playing was very impressive. He strode into the control room with a real cocky air and said, "Did I tell you I was the drummer for Steeleye Span?" I felt a bit of a pratt having not known this but it was however the best months I had ever spent doing what could be termed work.

*MASTER and APPRENTICE.*

Nigel was very tough as an engineer. He bollocked me for taking too long on the guitar, he constantly told me to re-do vocal takes. He taught me how to work in a studio. Most of the time he hardly charged me, or charged me for fewer hours than we were doing. I admired him tremendously and will always be grateful for what he gave me...a 'Producer's mentality in the recording studio.

Two of his friends Mark Williamson and Vince Cross, bass and keyboards respectively, joined in, again for no payment. We had an agreement whereby they would get a percent if things began to happen but they did it out of the goodness of their hearts. It was a joy making Nocturn Gate, I truly wished it would not be my only album. A couple of months and Nocturn Gate was finished. 10 tracks, all originals.

Calling on the lovely Karen again, we made the recordings into a 12" vinyl album. My sister completed the artwork for me one night. She is quite an amazing talent, being an artist, paste up artist Oh, and she has a few maths degrees too.

*ABBEY ROAD ST JOHN'S WOOD*

One of the procedures in the vinyl days was to 'Final Mix' recordings onto a vinyl master or 'Lacquer' Basically this means playing the tape connected to a recording lathe, this then transmitted the recording onto the vinyl. This was then the master, which in turn is then used to grow stampers. The master lacquer is then magnetised in a tank with a low electrical current, metallic flakes attach themselves to the master and form a stamper, which is then used to press the record into long sheets of hot vinyl. I've always found this process interesting. There are very few 'Lathes' around. S.R.T. used the one at Abbey Road, the EMI studios in North London and I was allowed to go and oversee this 'Final Mix'

The sound engineer running the lathe in the early 80's was Nick Webb. Nick and I instantly became friends. He knew of Nigel Pegrums work, was an avid guitarist having worked with many legends over his years in Abbey Road, including the 'Beatles'. He wanted to know all aspects of the project with S.R.T. And as I would find out over the years, always, gave the best sound on the lacquers from the master tapes, which were always held on quarter inch reel to reel tape. Many times over the years I would visit Abbey Road Studios, either on business or just because I was passing.

Now I had to find distribution. If someone in Manchester heard a radio performance and went into a record shop to order the record, its the distribution companies, not the record labels that the record shops will deal with. The Major Record labels usually have their own distribution company. RCA's is in Birmingham now, EMI I think is in Swindon Wilts but the smaller labels go through 'The Independents'. The big ones then were; Pinnacle, Rough Trade, and PRT. The latter had been known as PYE Records, but in the deal with 'Phillips' they'd sold all rights to the name 'PYE', in the domestic appliance sell off, so now they just used the trading name 'P.R.T.', which stood for Precision Records and Tapes.

I had traipsed around most of these and many smaller companies. I'd written and sent tapes to them, getting negative responses. Not a 'No', just 'we can't be bothered' attitude. I was getting a bit frustrated so I parked myself in the reception of P.R.T. asking to see the manager, telling the receptionist inaccurately, they wanted to see me. This was a little lie....well it was a big'un....But the ploy worked. John Morton came down to see me. They listened again, after some deliberation, they agreed to take 'Nocturn Gate' on my own record label – 'Ooze Records' for distribution. The contracts were signed over the next few weeks and we were in business!!!

Not only was the deal a brilliant one, they'd agreed to handle ALL future pressing costs and give me all but 27% of the trade price from the shops. John Morton also became a close friend. The term 'close friend' might sound over-used in these pages but it's true. Most of my friends ARE from the music industry. I think a lot of people brand the music industry as being full of 'unreal' people. While this obviously has some bearing, the majority of people I worked with throughout my entire musical career have been very good to me and are the type of people I love sitting in a pub chatting to. Most of those mentioned I still see on a regular basis if a bit sporadic.

But now it was back to the plugging of the radio stations properly. The United Kingdom at that time had approximately 50 Independent Local Radio stations. They were dotted all around the country, with big ones in the major cities. They held a lot of sway with audiences. Radio One was the biggest but the ILR's have their place in the scheme of things. I started targeting these ILR's all over England and Wales, sending them to Scotland. We were now getting airplay and the album 'Nocturn Gate' was slowly starting to sell.

I began pushing the stations for Interviews on air, many agreed to do this. They were very interested in the way I'd marketed this new album on an own label, which was usually the talking point on air. The very first interview I attended was one night in Nottingham for 'Trent Radio'. The Evening DJ who's name escapes me was great. His girlfriend escorted me into the building, chatted about how things were going with the new album and also happened to be very intelligent and knowledgeable about the media in general. (I hadn't even noticed she was a very attractive blonde with very long legs and a Hell of a figure!) I was taken into the studio and I talked for neigh on two hours on air with her boyfriend the DJ. It was a good start and I left feeling things were really going well.

A short time later I was horrified to learn that same DJ was on the front page of the national papers. He had shot the girlfriend...and then himself!

The BBC had been treating me very well. I had the first play with Peter Powell and the producers were receptive to this 'Own Plugging' attempt. The security at the BBC was not so tough as it is now but you still had to have a form of pass. I had all the documentation to go freely about the Langham Place and the Western House buildings. Radio One worked on a strict method of appointments, you phoned a producer at a certain time in the week, if you were lucky, you got the appointment. Once in the building, they were ok with me going around, leaving copies of the album on producers and broadcast assistants desks. I walked into Dave Atkey's office to leave an album, Janice Long was seated at the desk. She said hello and asked about the album I was leaving. I quickly offered her a copy, she read the sleeve etc and wanted to know more. I told her about being a Fireman, being in the hospital etc. "You want to push that angle more, you have to use what you can in this business" she said. I thought about it a lot. So many times publicity is gained for a secondary reason to the item, be it book or record, that you are trying to get noticed. She had a point.

'Nocturn Gate' made a profit with UK sales, getting a big boost with a number of exporters who bought them for Germany, we were in the black with the album!

We were now getting airplay all over the UK. PRT became more involved, John Morton asked me if I had any ideas regarding what to do next? He suggested I return to the recording studio to do some more recordings. He even offered (and I did not realise at this time how 'Big' an offer this was) for PRT to foot the bill for all recording costs.

Back to 'Pace Studios' and I began work on two tracks, one original and a cover of Cream's 'White Room' I'd always wanted to do this, have always loved the track, still perform it today in the 'Live Set'. I had plans for a string sound over the top of the main guitar riff. Nigel thought brass...We used brass. It did work well. We ended up putting just about every sound possible on it, synth's pianos even tympani drums courtesy of synth technology. The sound was big and it was intended as an EP.

I took the finished master down to PRT and was ushered into the office as I had been previously. They put the track on the tape player......There was an instant reaction from both John Morton and his boss Ian Holloway. Ian walked over to the hi fi and turned it up full....'THIS IS BLOODY FANTASTIC BEN" their mood toward me changed significantly, I was offered drinks, asked if I wanted to be taken out for a meal? John Morton then said "This is too big for your own label Ben, we'll take it over from here, this is magic. It will go out on the PRT label"

I was literally launched into orbit, totally on a high from the reaction, we'd taken the next big step. I had to phone someone. As I left the building I used the phone box across the street, (yes boys and girls, there once was a time before mobile phones!) I could hear 'White Room' blaring out of the 4$^{th}$ floor window of the P.R.T. headquarters, this was turning out to be a pretty good day!

I called Sharon, I called Nigel Pegrum at Pace telling them both what had just happened in the PRT headquarters. (I think I even told the telephone operator, but she wasn't too interested!) Nigel countered "that's great Ben, but calm down till we've got the money and the full go ahead, record companies have a habit of doing this and not delivering"....He was right. Over the coming 3 months whenever I called PRT to see what was happening. There was a stalling attitude, my enthusiasm began to sink.

I did bring out one more item with the 'Ooze Record' label, a seven inch single titled 'See Me Cry'. Not from the album, it was a one off I had recorded with Nigel's friend Mark Williamson. Mark had taken over from Nigel Pegrum while 'Steeleye Span' were on a tour of Australia. Mark was an excellent singer and backing singer, pulling out vocal arrangements from nowhere and making the backing vocals like another instrument altogether. He did like to use more modern techniques than Nigel. This track had at one point, a drum machine supplying percussion. I didn't like it, Mark wanted it to stay so we ended up having two versions.

Back to Radio One with this single, (which had the 'real drum' version) and again I did manage to get some airplay with it, on the late evening slot with Richard Skinner. While visiting the Langham Place building to see his producer, I walked out of the building and headed toward the 'All Souls Church' in Portland Place. A couple of mean looking 'Dudes' pulled up to the Radio One door on I think, a Kawasaki 750, it was green, the usual colour of that make. These two 'Toughies, dressed in leather took off their helmets, the rider of the bike was 'Alison Moyet', her pillion passenger had been her 'Yazoo' partner 'Vince Clarke'. No one believed me when I re-told this incident to people, maybe Miss Moyet will confirm it one day!!


Now this is a portion of the story I'm still not sure how to tell. I'm not sure what was in my mind
Even though the PRT situation was less than ideal, things had still been happening. Radio stations
were calling and asking if anything new was coming out by Ben Markus.
All I can say was, while not giving up, we moved the family to Devon and to this day I'm not sure
why. I think....I say think...I started getting a bit scared, I was still only a year or so away from the
crisis with the brain tumour scenario. It was a wrong move, but I did it. We became Devon exiles.
Not a lot happens with the music scene in Devon...... trust me!

*LIVE AID 85.*

We moved into our Devon house on the day the Live Aid concert was held at Wembley Football Stadium. I should've been doing housey type things but I was watching all the acts, taping what I could for prosperity (I only had one or two videotapes) and was already starting to feel like I was 'out of the party'. We'd still not unpacked and Sharon was pregnant with our 2$^{nd}$ child but I just had to watch all of it, there would never be another like it.

On February 18$^{th}$ 1986 JULIA EMILY MARKUS came into the world, pretty much as she's lived her life, adorable and aggressive. She was if memory serves, nearly 9 lbs. The labour had not been easy for Sharon, having been rushed into hospital a few times with Brackson Hicks Contractions. Now it was snowing, the roads were closing down. I had an old Range Rover so I could make sure we got to the tiny Cottage Hospital in Tiverton Devon, problem was...the doctor couldn't.

One nurse was on duty and she was having to deal with 2 women in labour. I had undergone training for emergency childbirth with the Fire Service, so I'm proud to say, Sharon and I coped more or less on our own throughout the birth. It went pretty quick once her waters broke despite the initial problems. Now we had 2 little girls to bring up, I thought I would have to settle down now and forget music.

Her birth was the not the only time Julia scared the pants off us. Easter 1987 she became really sick, vomiting constantly, you could tell she had a blinding headache. The doctor became very concerned and was coming out every 3 to 4 hours to check on her, this made us both aware that they were worried about Meningitis. After the third or forth visit by the GP, he said on the Easter Sunday, "I don't like the look of her, I think you'd better take her into hospital". Most of you will know how hard it is to drive slowly in circumstances of this nature but you just have to. We arrived at around 2-o clock in the afternoon. Julia was put on the children's ward. She was only just over a year, normally fully mobile but not today. The ward doctors decided to take spinal fluids via a Spinal Tap for which she had to remain conscious for this very painful procedure. She was clamped into a bed and the needle inserted into her spine to draw the jelly like substance to check for the notorious disease. The first one didn't work, so the poor little toddler had to suffer a second attempt. By now her crying was getting the better of her stamina and she just became quiet, this worried me more than when she was noisy. Julia was in a dreadful state however the tests proved she had a lesser strain that the hospital termed 'Menningism'. The Home Office did still have to be informed but Julia made (what we thought at the time) was a full recovery. However it is more than likely this episode as a 14-month-old baby was the factor that bought about diabetes when she was 9 yrs old but she came home within 2 weeks and returned to full health. She did however, scream when anyone with a white coat came near her for months afterwards.

Julia was 2 years old when my mother, who she looked so much like, passed away. It was January 1988. My mother had a keen sense of humour and was a stylish lady. All that was on the death certificate was Myocardial infarction, which I believe, means her heart stopped working. Again, like my father, she had smoked for the bigger part of her life

I could not forget the idea of doing something more in music and the fact I had left the Home Counties just at the time when it looked like major label money had been on the table. Knowing I could've done more, it was bothering me. I formed a Band in Devon, we rehearsed quite a bit but venues to play at were very thin on the ground, especially in the winter months.

So I started writing again, the idea was for another album. CD's were now becoming common place, although we never had a CD player at this time. They were now as popular maybe more so, than vinyl. I knew CD it would have to be if we were going to sell any. I put the finance together for 'JUST A SHAGGY DOG STORY', the name chosen because we had at that time, a very ragged, very bolshi Old English Sheepdog called 'Sam'. I thought the photos for the sleeve would look great with him on it, getting him to pose however was a completely different matter. The day Sam was to become a leading model we washed and cleaned our 4 yr old Sheepdog. He didn't seem to go a lot on that... The minute he jumped out of the car near where the photos would be taken, he found the biggest pile of crap he could and rolled in it. God that dog was a Git!

The song-writing for 'Dog Story' was going well. 'White Room' would be included and I thought at the time, should be the single. Nigel agreed to do the honours at his Pace Studios. Previously Pace was a 16 track during the 'Nocturn Gate' recording but had now been uprated to a 24track analogue with an Otari multi track running on two inch tape and another lovely big desk. (I know size shouldn't matter....but it does with mixing desks!)

I had also written a song that just couldn't be sung by a male, it was much softer than my previous

33

material and I wrote it with a female in mind. I didn't know anyone who could manage it but Nigel did. Melanie Harrold aka Joanna Carlin offered to do lead vocals for 'All I Know'. We talked on the phone a couple of times, I think I played the song over the phone for her so she could get a feel for it and not be completely in the dark over how I wanted it sung. On the day she came in to record the track she was Magic. She had the feel, the emphasis all spot on. 'All I know' was and still is, many people's favourite song from 'Shaggy Dog Story'. Melanie, my Melanie, still wants to do a version of this track, maybe the next album???

I also wanted to diversify in sound. I had loved the original 'Chicago Transit Authority' recordings, the way the brass joined with rock tracks. I know the Beatles are credited with starting this but Chicago took it to another level. I was using a sax player in Devon, Alison Sumner who was also working on backing vocals for 'Shaggy Dog Story'. She knew Rick Taylor, well known in brass circles for trombone playing. He had been behind Elton John on the 'Live Aid' stage in 85, so when she asked if he'd be interested, he immediately said yes.

I sent some tapes and he suggested I bring the master reel (2 inch reel to reel tape that contained all the instruments in a way they could be altered, i.e. in the mix etc) and join him in Newcastle. He knew of a good studio that used STUDER's and we could put some 'Real' brass on.

'Angelene' was the prime track I wanted the arrangement on, if we had time, I would also get him to have a crack at 'You'll never Know' a BB King song I wanted to cover. Rick very kindly put me up for the night at his and his wife's house. On the drive into Newcastle the following day I noticed he smoked quite a lot of the funny stuff. I have to say I have NEVER used any type of substance but many do in this line up work. I think my spell in the 'National' had the effect of making me feel and live a bit differently. I didn't drink and had not been drunk since I was 17 and I stopped smoking when I was 30. As I said, the spell in the London hospital cured me of a lot of things.

Rick virtually chain smoked 'Shit'! I never could stand the smell and it does affect me quite a lot. I had a BMW 735 with a sunroof, (that first album was good financially for us!). On the trip into Newcastle City it was....pissing down! (See first chapter....weather trends for the UK!)
I had to get some fresh air, I just had to open the sunroof, it was peeing down and we were both getting drenched. We turned up at the 'Lynx Recording studios utterly soaked. I said to Rick "Don't you think you smoke that stuff rather a lot?" "I never have anything stronger nowadays, I never snort any more" he replied....and he wasn't joking!.

One track was going badly, I just couldn't get into it and I thought I would have to abandon it. It didn't seem to fit, the lyrics were wishy washy, I couldn't see where it was going. So I just left it and considered starting something else from scratch.

Our next door neighbour in Devon was Anne. She had two daughters, the elder was away in Germany working as a translator. Alison and Rachel loved our little girls and came around quite often. On returning home from school one afternoon Rachel, the younger of the two, knocked on our door. "Have you seen Mum?"
"No, not all day Rachel". This in itself was not untoward, but I could see Rachel was worried. I followed the young girl back into her house, the place was empty. I went into the garage, Anne's ageing Honda Civic stood there, a layer of exhaust related smudge covered the garage and the smell of exhaust smell was everywhere. The car's engine had long stopped, I shouted to Rachel to go inside and bellowed for Sharon to help. I had attended a few incidents like this and although I hoped it would end happily, I was pretty sure what I was going to find.

Anne had been there for hours, rigour mortise had set in, there was nothing I or anyone could do. She had left a note by her side. I quickly scanned the pages in case there was any blame she was going to attach to her daughters in her altered frame of mind. You never know what anyone in a disturbed frame of mind might say, had I found any such blame, I would have destroyed the letters there and then. In cases like this I don't mind lying to the authorities!
But thankfully, there was no blame proportioned to anyone. She, like many other people in the modern world, was just very unhappy and could not face another day!

To say Rachel and Alison were grief stricken is an understatement. Rachel more or less stayed with us for 3 to 4 months before going to live with relatives in another part of the country. Alison returned home within hours her face as she got out of the taxi was indescribable. I for once seemed at a loss for words. Alison also stayed with us in the weeks that followed. The 6 of us going for many days out in and around the South West in a bid to re-focus Alison and Rachels attention from the past weeks, this was right in the middle of the SHAGGY DOG STORY recording spell.

I began writing the lyric for what would be called 'Can't go back' It was directed at Alison and her younger sister Rachel. When she heard the finished song, Alison burst into tears. What I failed to say with words, I managed to say in the song. Every time I hear it now it still carries and will always carry a mixed emotion.

Throughout the recording back in Milton Keynes, Nigel very kindly offered me a room at his and his wife Carmel's place. One evening after recording he was sitting in his study, I stood at the door, at his indication I came in. On the wall were a number of Gold Albums. 5 or 6 I think, albums awarded to 'Steeleye Span' for records sold over the years and all over the world. I suppose I looked a bit like a little kid looking at Fire Engines again. He said "You know I'm more proud of the material I've produced with you than with Steeleye" It seemed hard to believe but I knew from his face it was true.

Within weeks I had the master, 'Just a Shaggy Dog Story' was a reality, time to find distribution. I called up PRT again, John Morton agreed to see me right away, he said they would take the new album but hinted the company was not in a good shape, further indicating I'd be wise to look elsewhere. That was a great shame for the company and for me. I really liked John and trusted him. PYE Records had been a big company but big companies were in the throws of going down the pan in the music industry. It was the end of the 80's and the financial world was in crisis. Many more record companies and indeed companies in general, would be bankrupt before the next 3 years were over.

Pinnacle Distribution agreed to take the new 'White Room' single and 'Just a Shaggy Dog story' album. CD production could not this time, be done with S.R.T., they had not yet caught up with the CD revolution, they would but not for a year or two.

Then Pinnacle did the dirty on me. After the first batch of singles were pressed, George Kimpton Howe called and just said "Sorry we can't do your stuff" I had had a firm yes from him, but nothing in writing!

When you've got this far with something and someone drops you in it, you do tend to panic a little and choose the first life raft you see. Trouble was, the next life raft was full of holes and I'd be better off swimming! (I'd be better off bloody drowning!!!)

36

I hawked the new album around the usual distribution companies. The mandatory indifference shining like a beacon of sludge in the most creative of industries. It came down to two companies who would take it; 'Jetstar' which was run by Mr Carl Palmer and 'Supertrack' which was run by Ian Holloway. Jetstar was known mainly for reggae but Carl Palmer wanted to break into the 'Rock' market. He liked 'Shaggy Dog Story' and wanted to do a distribution deal. While Ian Holloway formerly of PRT knew me and also wanted the album. He had started his own Supertrack Records. I knew Ian and I thought things might be better with someone you know than someone you don't. All the discussions were dealt with over the phone. I can remember Ian telling me "Carl Palmer is good with Reggae but this is more my line" I agreed and signed the contracts by post.

I was in London for some reason or another and had to drop off the first bits of artwork for the sleeve and booklet with Supertrack. He had offices in Bloemfontein Ave W12, I thought quite a good area for business.

I drove up and down Bloemfontein, it was terraced houses, no sign of anything that resembled a record company. I must have the wrong street. Back to the A –Z, checked my paperwork. No, this is it. I stopped outside 5 Bloemfontein Ave, knocked on the door and waited. An oldish woman answered the door. "I'm looking for Supertrack Records, you don't know where it is do you Mam?"

She didn't say a word, just motioned for me to follow her through her house. (It was a mid-terrace) she led me out of the back door while her ageing dog was barking at me, letting me know I was an intrusion to his peace and there it stood.... SUPERTRACK RECORDS.....A garden shed at the rear of 5 Bloemfontein Avenue. My heart sunk!! Really sunk....I was screwed. There had been a storm the night before and the roof to the garden shed had come down. Ian Holloway was inside with a hair dryer, drying out bits of paper that looked for the life of me like Record Contracts!!!

There was a lot of water around.. I said to him "I wouldn't use that hair dryer with all this water around". He sheepishly looked back but didn't say too much.

Maybe it'll be all right I thought. We went ahead with everything as planned, I had no choice, I'd signed the contract, I couldn't stop now. He did have an umbrella deal with EMI. That is to say Supertrack would be allocated sales space within the massive EMI infrastructure. EMI would handle ALL logistics of sending out the cassettes and CD's to the shops. Supertrack Records just dealt directly with the labels. The donkey work would all be accomplished by EMI.

'Just a Shaggy Dog Story' was received well, by the radio and the press. This review clip came from 'Hi Fi News and Record Review 1990. Ken Kessler wrote;

*If just once a year a treasure like this pops up then it's all been worthwhile. MARKUS and crew have a perfect grasp of the art of Pop and RNB, unlikely bedfellows to be sure. Which puts the compositions right up there with – nobody. It's too earthy and soulful to classify with sixties revivalists and too bright and catchy to bunch with head down muso's. A1 \*\*\* deserved here!*

That was one of the best, if not the best review I'd had, at least until that point. The 'Our Price' chain of stores were now buying 'Shaggy Dog'. The single 'Angelene' was played on 56 of the local radio stations, Radio One played it, Radio Two played it. Sir Simon Hornby of W.H. Smiths wrote to me personally to congratulate me on a splendid album and the business expertise to get it made and marketed. The amount of radio airplay awarded to the single over a given time meant I was promoted to Assoc Member with the P.R.S. (Performing Rights Society, a society of composers). Jennifer Warnes manager had also contacted me one night by fax, he wanted a copy of 'All I know' for Ms Warnes. I still don't know to this day if she recorded it or not.

It looked like we might make some more money with 'Shaggy Dog'. The BMW was a few years old, maybe time for a new one. I went to the local Devon Mercedes showroom to look at a couple of 2 yr old 420's. They were nice. I was, as usual, dressed in a leather jacket. Don't you just hate condescending car salesmen, they sneer at you as if to say, "You can't afford this you scruffy bastard!" One such type started his patronising routine, the radio was tuned to the local 'Devon-air Radio'. I recognise that starting riff on guitar!!! "Hear that Pal? That's my latest album they're playing!!!" I continued (after shouting for Melanie and Sharon to come and listen to the radio) "Mercedes are a bit common.....think I'll go look at the Bentleys now!!" The salesman tried to look indifferent......he didn't manage it very well!

During the promoting for 'Shaggy Dog' Melanie began accompanying me more and more. I suppose she was always my Hoppo, Julia was later on as well when she grew up. One visit to Radio One building in W1,Melanie was with me. I saw the Head of Music Chris Lycett, his son Danny was there on a holiday job. Chris offered for Danny to show my 8 yr old daughter around Radio

One. She met Gary Davis, Mike Read (who wanted her to join him in the control room while he was on air but she got a little bit of stage fright there and declined) and finally Danny and Clair in reception showered her with tee shirts, sweat-shirts, and all the Goodies that could be had. I know it made her day special. She even stood side by side with Kylie Mynogue in the reception area, (Mel was I think, taller, Kylie is small). Things have been tight financially speaking in later years, I hope the days like that one made up for it in some way.

About this time. SEAN GEOFFREY MARKUS weighed in at around 8 lbs on MARCH 22$^{nd}$ 1990. The birth was fairly easy and for the third time I was the first to hold a 'Baby Markus'.....I wonder if this one will play guitar???

It was looking very very good!. My reservations about the Supertrack set up had gone away for a while at least. The CD's were being sold, we'd already made a profit with the initial sales, more needed pressing. My royalties from the first batch would not be paid for another 4 months so I had to get a fairly large loan to pay for the pressing and promotion. We used the house in Nth Devon as collateral, at the time it was valued at £110,000. We owed less than £20,000 on the mortgage so we thought we were completely safe, if all else failed we could sell the house to get out of trouble.....Property had NEVER lost its value!!!

I wonder how many people said that in 1989-1991!!

You know what's coming. Supertrack never paid a penny to Citation Records (my record label) for 'Shaggy Dog' sales at the time of the sales (although a token payment was forthcoming after much verbal fighting but long after the initial sales had taken place). The loans were defaulted on, the money needed to finance going around the country for the promotion of the album was growing. The figure for the extra pressing just added to this, we had to promote the album in order to get noticed. That meant going to London just about every week, we ran up a huge loan and credit card debt. Just to help along the drop in our house price, RAF Chivenor in Nth Devon closed down, hundreds of houses were on the market. The Government was selling the homes and RAF staff who until then, usually bought homes off the base, were now conspicuous by their absence!! It was Shit hitting the fan time!!

To add insult to injury, I later found out from a friend who'd been travelling, that he'd seen 'Just a

39

shaggy dog story' for sale in Hong Kong. Seems someone was bootlegging it there. I did receive some airplay royalties for HK Radio but I never knew who was selling my album.

Chapter 7

*I HATE BANKS!!*

Its not a bankist thing, not an ageist thing. Its not based on any pre-conceived inner twistedness, I just hate the Banks!! The Midland bank, so happy to give us the money to cover the pressing, were now being awful about the trouble I found myself in. The manager became unhelpful indicating in a brusque manner that we were going to lose our house.

In the western world, the financial institutions seem to have become (or at least perceive themselves as) the new religion!!! It's fucking money.....that's all. It has no life force, it has no mind of its own........It's fucking pieces of paper......end of story!!!!!!

But it has come to dominate nearly every aspect of the way we live, breathe and raise our children. God I wish there was an easy way to go back to the barter system. People take jobs they hate, get addicted to the money and keep themselves locked into a prison that only they hold the key for. I'm not saying this because I have little of it. I've had lots of money and I've lived with very little. I once turned down $4.6 million to do something that wasn't illegal but I just wouldn't do!! So don't think this is 'sour grapes' it aint!

The populace in general is sucked in by this 'have to do well' frame of mind, taught from peers and parents that it's the only way to do things, they can ALL be excused. BUT THE BANKS!!!!! They act like they all know something we don't, that money is THEIR DOMAIN and we know Fuck All!!! They are condescending about how we spent it, what we buy, they think we are totally and utterly useless regarding its usage which THEY alone know! THEY would ALL love for a law to be passed that would mean they were the only people allowed near the stuff!!....God I HATE BANKS!!! Soapbox time over!!

So we had to find the money to pay off The Midland. Our other personal accounts were held with Lloyd's. We would have to borrow A LOT. It was the only way to at least keep the house for a while. We went and told the truth, the manager at Lloyds told us (and I know he'll refute this but Sharon was in the room and she'll back me up...because it's true!!)
You'll never get the loan for that reason, you'll have to make something up....I'll sign it!

We did and to this day we still owe for the money we lost over the loss of royalties from ' Shaggy

41

Dog Story'!  While certain other people were back in business in a very short time!!!

**\*\*WARNING\*\***

The above story is still a bit tender, if you see us at a gig  DON'T ASK ME ABOUT IT!!!

*TERRY BLOOD'S*

Well we lost a lot of royalties but 'Terry Bloods Distribution' of Newcastle under Lyme offered to step in and take over distribution but the momentum had slowed and our funds were getting frighteningly low.

One of my trips to the Radio One building  (still plugging singles from the album) I met up with a man I sort of recognised – 'Andy Price Watts'. As a teenager in a scruffy leather jacket, he was just Andy Watts, somewhere along the way the 'Price' had been added.

Andy was now a Plugger for record labels, and ran a record label, and a publishing company, and operated as a media publicist. The list seemed endless of the companies he was involved in, he offered to take over plugging for 'Shaggy Dog Story' and it wouldn't cost 'a lot'

No money changed hands in the agreement but he would, if he did anything, get publishers rights. (I was pretty low by now and would probably have agreed a deal with Arthur Daley had he been working in the music industry) Andy survived on Bullshit as a tool of the trade, trouble was he didn't know when to turn it off. He did try hard to get the album played but it was a losing battle. There were some harsh words exchanged for a time, but you can't stay mad at a bloke like Andy Price Watts for long.

Music was going to have to take a back seat, for a while at least. I seriously began to wonder if it really was all over with music, maybe for good.

42

There were very few jobs in Devon, the minute I opened my mouth and my Luton accent became evident, there were none! I'm not blaming Devonites! The minute the work situation gets bad, everyone hires closer to home, it's natural and I'd probably do the same if I were in their shoes.

It seemed a good time to move back to Bedfordshire, I have to admit that I missed Luton. Luton is sadly misunderstood. It has this bad name, which I'm sure the incidents that caused the name are true but it's no worse than any other big industrial town. You put lots of people in a small space.....they get pissed off!!!

Crime starts to happen but there has to be a balance somewhere.

I always liked Luton, so I found myself heading back to get a job to pay the Banks their weekly screw. Trouble was things were bad all over, not just Devon. Always a keen motorcyclist, I knew it would probably have to be as a motorcycle courier. I had some other skills other than squirting water around but they were in fields of work that were in the worst slump ever. Motorcycle courier it would be.

*A CARS!*

Geoff Millard has been my friend since I was 12 yrs old. He had a farm, a building business and a bed and breakfast facility on his land. He let me have lodgings virtually for nothing when I explained why I was coming back to Bedfordshire. The trip back was a baptism of Fire. I'd bought a BMW (never exciting but good workhorse) with the last of my cash and set off. It Pee'd down the entire journey. I've never been so wet, my gloves started to leak, my leather's started to leak and I think I took on 5 lb of body weight by osmosis! I arrived at Geoff and Maggie's looking very bedraggled. Next day I had found a job with ' A' Cars in Luton, the interview lasted about 30 seconds. "Can you ride a bike? Can you get commercial insurance? When can you start?" Were I think, the only questions he asked me.

You can, if you use your head, earn good money as a motorcycle courier. You have to follow a few basics though. Always keep a spare bike, always do the tax. (Tax always seems a lifetime away, its like Christmas in reverse but it always catches couriers out) and don't mess with London Taxi drivers. They hate motorcycle couriers. They'll try to knock you off, block your road just because you can get through the traffic with less fuss than they can and whenever possible, make your life much harder than it already is.

The bikers though really are great bunch. Many times I have pulled up to traffic lights in the middle of the Strand, or the Euston Rd and just started a conversation with another motorcycle courier. Within seconds anyone hearing us talking would think we knew each other, which of course was not the case. The most memorable incident for 'A Cars' occurred in the 'Old Kent Rd'. They were resurfacing the entire road, a mammoth job. I was pulled up at a pedestrian crossing, waiting for the lights to change. I was wearing old 'Fire boots', very water tight but they were made with no zips or fastenings so Firemen can slip into them easily. Trouble was you could also slip out of them pretty easily as well. Unknown to me, my feet were resting in hot tar just before the chippings were added. The lights changed and I pulled away, my foot felt a bit cold. The fire boot had come off and was stuck in the hot tar. A Pony Express rider saw this, stopped and laughed himself silly before he got off his bike and got my boot for me. I had stopped and was hopping around on one foot, I thanked him, (if in a sarcastic manner) and rode off covering the remaining yards to the 'drop'. Walking into the plush reception I walked up to the receptionist. She was looking behind me, I wondered what was holding her attention, I turned as well. About 15 very black footprints followed me right up to the desk, right over the very white carpet! "Right" the receptionist began "You're company will have to pay for that!" she continued "Which company do you work for?" "Pony Express" I replied and made a hasty getaway WITHOUT getting her to sign the docket for the delivery!

I was missing the family, Sharon came the couple of weekends I couldn't get down to Devon and we began looking at ways to move back. We just couldn't sell the house. (The stigma attached to this whole episode stopped me calling it a home) it would have to be a renting situation.

I'd been looking around but prices were high, Geoff helped as he was in the trade. Then I saw a huge old place in Wilstead, 5 bedrooms, a 30ft living room, a 25ft kitchen and equal size dining room! Great big land area front and back, it was directly in the front of an Industrial unit but that was fine by me. The décor wasn't bad either, not great but we could do a lot there. I immediately loved it knowing Sharon and the children would too. They all did, the children ran around the empty house on our first inspection and literally jumped for joy at the possible games they could play in such a big home, we planned the move and came back.

There was plenty of work and plenty of places to work, strange during a recession but it always seems to be that way if you can ride a bike.

Woody knew I was back, 'Lets start a live Band'! I can't remember if I asked him or he asked me, I immediately put some adverts into the local papers to get things moving on the 'Live' front. The Wilstead house was plenty big enough to re-hearse in, every Sunday morning we would meet, some of the Band often staying for a buffet lunch afterwards. All the children loved to sit and listen to our progress. Melanie more so than her siblings, she was obviously thinking she would like to be involved too. We put together a set list, half-and-half Covers and Originals. Took a while to get the boys out live but we did it. Steve Woodward, Pete Lubbock, Jay Alibone, Steve Foggin, John Morrey, Ian Paul, all played at one time or another with 'The Markus Band' and rehearsed on a Sunday morning at 46 Luton Road Wilstead.

*PRESS THE BARRY McGUIRE BUTTON*

I may have said previously, I never really liked my voice on my early recordings. I once said to Nigel Pegrum during mixing. "Have'nt you got a button somewhere you can press that makes me sound like Barry McGuire?" (Eve of Destruction) I always liked his voice, as a solo artist and with The New Christy Minstrels. It was the type of voice I longed for.

During one of those sunny halcyon days spent taking motorcycle trips to the English Capital City to pleasantly chat with passing cab drivers on the streets, I had an altercation with one of those pleasant chaps aboard his shiny black stead!!

It was resolved fairly quickly, but I had a broken rib and had caught a blow to the throat. I could feel my throat tightening on the way home. That night it got worse.. 2 days later I sounded like JAMES BROWN!!

Did I call my doctor? did I attend hospital? Nope, I booked a recording studio!!! thinking 'If this voice is going to last a couple of days I'm getting full use from it!!'. I had started to record 3 songs in a local 16 track studio in Bedford. So with my voice now sounding very different, I took the master tape to Nigel Mills over at 'Audio Labs' in Buckingham and re-did the vocals. "Christ Ben, you weren't kidding, your voice has bloody changed hasn't it?" Was Nigel's comment...."Too bloody right Pal, so lets work quickly before it goes!!" I replied.

I think I over did the gravely style at first but my voice has stayed with that husky texture to this day. I try to balance it out a bit better now but for a spell I did EVERYTHING gravely! Even the ballads!!

We were playing on a regular basis but I still longed to do some more serious recording. I had the material, I managed to keep in touch with the 'People' I knew in the capital. More often than not, just popping in during motorcycle forays into London. Ray Jenks of 'Castle Records' then of B.M.G. Records has always been interested and told me to send him anything and everything I had. I had a strange relationship with Rupert Perry the Man Dir at the time of EMI. We exchanged many letters, he liked what I was doing, said it many times in his letters. I just couldn't get him to sign the band or me but to be honest, he was always encouraging, always sent back something positive regarding what we were doing., I never met him but he was a 'Gent'

His secretary and pa I did meet on more than one occasion though. No Dolly bird was Marian Back. She held the position because I'm guessing she ran the whole company. She would always write or talk on the phone. One day on a motorcycle in London I stopped in at the old EMI building in W1. Melanie sometimes came on the back if it was a sunny day. We went into the reception of 22 Manchester Square, Marian told the receptionist to let us up to the 4th floor where she gave us both tea and biscuits and we chatted at length. Nothing to do with music, just general chit chat sort of stuff. I did this a couple of times whenever I had a minute to spare here and there. One day she called me at home out of the blue and asked if I had been in London and was I popping in again? I

46

had cut down the courier work, for my health if nothing else. I said I would call in when I came to London again but I never did...I heard Marion died of cancer a few months later. I should've realised she wanted to see me. I was too wrapped up in my own little world to hear what she was saying. I'm sorry Marian, truly sorry.


*EVER SEEN A BRASS MONKEY CRY?*


Melanie had been playing flute for quite a while, I can remember thinking the first few times I had heard her playing "I didn't think playing a flute was easy?" I had a few goes.....It wasn't. Melanie had the ability to pick out melodies, she heard and copied more or less what she heard. She was good, so good after a short spell she was good enough to play with the Band. I have always liked the sound of flute with Rock, it does blend in well.


She rehearsed with the various line ups usually picking out a riff to play over the top of the basic melody. It always worked well, managing to cut through a lot of the production due to its high pitch.


Geoff Millard was holding an outside celebration for his and his wife's 40th. They asked the Band to play for the night, it would be held in a cow barn which he converted nicely and was quite a decent sight when all finished and the 6,000 watt PA arrived. It would be Melanie's first Gig. Still just 13, she didn't seem to be suffering first time nerves, opposite to me for that night, I hate playing to crowds of people I know, they're always worse than an unknown audience.


It was held at the end of October, the day had been very sunny and quite mild but when night came it obviously began to get colder, much colder. The band were all sat in their cars with heaters on full, trying to keep themselves warm. The guitars were going out of tune, my hands were freezing, Christ I wished we'd been inside, too late now though.


We all mounted the makeshift stage with steamy vapour coming out of our mouths. The line up that night was; Myself guitar/vocals. Peter Lubbock guitar.

Steve Foggin drums. Keith Green bass, Jay Alibone tenor sax. Ken Blowhard alto sax (I cannot for the life of me remember the alto saxes name!) and my eldest daughter Melanie Markus on flute. She looked stunning in a dark coat and a scarf wrapped around her shoulders. She played fantastically many people that night commented on the future diva's performance. But for most of the band, we just wished it would end so we could go home and get warm.

*MY OWN WORST ENEMY!*

There have been many times over the years people of influence have taken note of what I and the various bands have been doing. A lot of money has been offered to do various projects, some I've took, some I've not. I have always seemed to attract attention from the major record labels with huge success promised.

The first such offer was from A & M RECORDS as previously mentioned. One of the sticking points was the fact they hinted at changing my style of music. I probably overreacted to this but I was young. Had I been a few years older I may have been a bit easier to consider change, or maybe just agreed and made sure things were done how I wanted in the first place. However....I dug my heels in. I am not sorry now, I think what will be will be but I probably was regarded by most of the record company executives as a 'Pain the in ass'.

In fact one Managing Director once labelled me 'His favourite pain in the ass'

Laurie Crow of CBS later SONY records was very keen to get an album of mine out with the CBS group of companies.

I was invited to the Aylesbury offices, given the guided tour by his assistant, offered the customary drinks/food etc. Then we sat down to discuss business.

Laurie's assistant then asked me who my Manager was. At this time I had no one in that position and no one I could even bullsh** about. The assistant who's name escapes me then said "You have to have a manger, if you've not got one....we shall appoint one to you". It was almost like being back at school listening to this crap from yet another record company underling. I replied with my vocal tone starting to take on a confrontational edge. "Well I've not got one and I don't relish the idea of having someone who knows nothing about the music I'm making coming on the scene and begin to tell me how to do things!"

I know I over did it, CBS did not take the material and no album was ever made with their company. I'm not really sorry either......just occasionally when I try to pay the bills!

Chapter 8

*WHAT'S THE DIFFERENCE BETWEEN A GUITARIST AND AN ANNUITY?*

Now my friends, if you are a bit put off by 'Boy' stuff, by people who collect 'Things' (I find most women in this category) then I would ask you to bear with this chapter. I'm told by someone who knows, it shows my passion clearly but it might be a bit heavy especially if you're not a guitarist.

I love guitars! I love acoustics, semi-acoustic electrics, solid-bodied electrics. I love Fenders, old and new, I love Epiphones old and new and I especially love 'Gibsons' old, knackered, brand spanking. I know why the '59' Humbucker was allegedly better than the '60' (Seth Lover when he invented the device, was putting approx 9,000 winds per coil on the humbuckers and then applied for a patent on the guitar pick-up. When the patent was granted by the US Patent office, The Gibson factory decided 7,500 winds per coil would be sufficient for the electrics and give enough power. See....I told you it would be boring!!!)

I can spend hours, nay days in guitar shops in the Home Counties, London, up north, down south, anywhere. The staff are usually very genuine, they share the love of the instrument. (However, every now and then you will come across a certified 'Ass hole', he'll think he's the only person that can play a guitar and will do his utmost to intimidate you....don't let him....You play how you want, just ignore the prick!!) I love picking up certain guitars, seeing whether or not the guitars like me. Two guitars made on the same day in the same factory can feel, play and sound so different in comparison to each other.

In 1988 I had seen an advert in one of the guitar mags, Gibson were bringing out a new '59 Re-issue' Line. I was using a 1959 Les Paul Special at the time. I'd had had it a few years but people were telling me that even this lesser model was becoming worth a bit in value. (I say lesser because the 'Les Paul Gold Tops' and 'Stds' were the premium and 'Customs' were nearly out of everyone's price range.) So I sold the '59' to a local guy and went along to 'Guitar World' in Bristol to try out one of these new '59 Re-issues, phoning a week or so before, they said a shipment was due in. We set off, Sharon and Julia came with me, Melanie was now at school. I played a couple of new 'Customs', a few 'Standards' but one in particular really felt like it wanted to come home with me. It was a 1988 'Standard', a gorgeous cherry sunburst with a definite aura or 'feel' about it. Classed as a 'CMT' or 'Carved Maple Top', it had a composite body of mahogany and maple. These were only going to be made for 3 yrs and in no time at all, were starting to rise in price just as the full blown 59 Re-issues did.

The sound from this guitar was supreme, due in no small way to the 'Genuine 59 re-issue pick-ups they used for 1988 on ALL the Gibson range. You could get the soft sounds, the harsh sounds when over driven, it was a dream. Quite a few 'Known' guitarists have commented on it over the years. I've done my best licks in the recording studio with this guitar. It was paid for with the money my mother left for me so it also had an emotional aspect to it and meant more than other guitars I had owned.

I've had 'Rickenbackers' (lovely to look at, not so powerful as some though but easy to play) 'Fender Stratocasters', my favourite was a 1977 Sunburst. I know the micro tilt 3 bolt necks aren't supposed to be good but this particular instrument was great. It was nicer to play than the 1957 model I had had 15 years earlier, although to be fair I did not know how to set up a guitar then and it may have been a teensy bit bad in the intonation stakes and had also been generally mucked about with.

I love the sound of a 12 string, electric or acoustic. I am still hankering for a 'Gibson' SG double neck 6 & 12. I tried one on a few months ago but it was so bloody heavy. You have to lean back on stage with that one but I like the versatility of what you can do, especially live. (You can always swap around in the studio from one to the other!)

I love amplifiers too, Fenders, Marshall's, Vox!

I used to, as mentioned in Chapter 1, use VOX amplifiers, but in 1983 at Machine Head music in Hitchin I saw a slightly used Marshall 100 MV (Master Volume). It had been orange but someone had painted it black. That amp head and speaker cab with 4x12 (G12-65's) has played every gig with me since 1983 until today, (Oct 2004). It's breezed through outside gigs, it's done London events, been pushed to its limit, played softly. In all that time I've changed one fuse (which I had lent to another guitarist in the Half Moon Putney one night when his fuse failed and I put it back in mine for it to blow the next time it was switched on) and one wheel assembly which failed. Even then 'Marshall's' at Bletchley Milton Keynes gave me one for free when I turned up to get the new one. That's service and it is 100% BRITISH.

I've never had a guitar say it had a headache, they always wanted to play! When you come home feeling Crap, there is NOTHING that compares to picking up an old 'Epiphone' semi-acoustic and just playing. If everyone played there would be no need for Counsellors. The World would be a better place, there'd be no wars! Well, maybe a few but you get the drift. (The world might get a teensy bit noisier though!)

Melanie always likes to strum her acoustic, Julia had a good run before she was diagnosed diabetic (blood testing 2 and 3 times a day results in pin pricking the fingers and makes them very sore, too sore to play). Sean would pick one up and begin to fall in love with them around his 11th birthday, just as his father did 30 years previously. It can be hard for many fathers to find common ground with sons, I have had it easy on this front. (And many others I have to agree) Every-time Sean and I are alone in a room or in the car, the conversation turns to guitars. I know we bore other people. Tough...he's my son. We'll talk about what we want!!

Looking for something to buy your offspring? It may not be the 'thing' for them but it's certainly worth the gamble!

Many times The Band will pull up at a music venue, there's an unspoken atmosphere between the different Bands. Who's biggest? Who should be topping the bill that night? etc etc. But even when this is in evidence, you'll usually find the guitarists of the different bands, breaking the ice, talking about who has what, who would like something different. "What's that model play like mate?" "Yea, have a go with this" It goes on and on. Its a common point of reference, it's fantastic. I've noticed dedicated vocalist can be the worst in these scenarios but guitarists usually ALWAYS find something to talk about regarding their love. "What's the difference between a Guitarist and an Annuity?" one Wag said to me holding his Fender Stratocaster in his lap as we all tuned up for the night! "An annuity will eventually mature and earn money!!!"

## Chapter 9

*MELANIE ROSE MARKUS*

So, with my new gravely voice I was wanting to make a full album with it. It was mid 90's, the live band was going ok, quite a few gigs here and there but a local Entertainment Agent, Andy Mason, who had taken a close interest in the Band and what we were doing told me, "If you go out a £200 pub band. You get treated like a £200 pub band!" I knew what he meant, its the 'Kings New clothes' syndrome. If the world sees you a certain way, it can be very hard if not impossible to break that perception, no matter what the reality is. I didn't want to have, or to be part of a £200 pub band!

My voice is ok, I can do certain types of music well, like the hard driving fast-ish Blues songs. I can handle the other stuff ok. If you buy 'Time to Move On' by 'Markus' and you really really should, it's a FANTASTIC ALBUM!! (this may sound like a plug....of course it is, I have to pay the Banks somehow!!), tracks like track 8 'You're alone', is my forte and also my favourite type of song but I like writing other types of music, the type of material that I'm not so hot at singing......

Wouldn't it be great to have a singer like Cher? No, better than Cher! Someone who could also perform the soft stuff with passion, someone who could belt out a Rock or Blues song with style and ability...Wouldn't it be Great???

I stumbled upon Melanie singing a Cher song, I think it was 'Jesse James'. The CD was on and Melanie was singing along to the recording. I was genuinely surprised at how good she sounded, I wasn't totally sure if I was hearing a strange echo and was mistaking my daughter's voice for Cher's and it just seemed like Melanie.

I got one of my acoustic guitars out of it's case and asked Melanie to sing a few songs. She was at first a bit sheepish but the power in my daughter's voice was, not only evident, it was bloody fantastic! As mentioned previously, Melanie had played with the band initially on flute. She was classically trained and also appeared in Youth Orchestra's but this was new. She did her first lead vocal on 'Rabble Without A Cause' in 1996. It was a promising start. She would get better though, much much better. For along time I thought it was just 'Proud Father' syndrome but others were starting to say and think the same thing.

*RABBLE WITHOUT A CAUSE.*

Rupert Cook owns a studio in Cranfield Bedfordshire called 'Lost Boys', he was a nice chap in his twenties and quite modern in outlook. I had done some re-mixing of some older tracks with him on which he did a very good job and improved them considerably. We talked at length and he offered to foot the bill for recording of a new album if I thought I could get a Record Label to sign the album. He did and I did.

Ray Jenks, now at B.M.G. Records Fulham London heard some of the first 'takes', called me one night as he was boarding a plane for New York saying he loved what we were doing and told me to call him on his return. He would do his utmost to get us signed to the BMG Record label, BMG was formerly known as R.C.A. Again things don't happen quite the way you think or plan but other record companies were interested in the 'Lost Boys Tapes'. Dave Bulmer of CM Records and Distribution also liked what he heard and told me to "Come up to Yorkshire and see him".

After talking with Dave we agreed on a deal and the percentage of the contract, how it would be marketed etc and how much we or 'I' would do to help the promotion along. Dave seemed impressed at how much I knew regarding promoting an album to the media. Things were looking up again. As I needed muso's more likely to do this full time, the line up changed a trifle, as in fact it has done many times over the years.

For 'Rabble Without a Cause' Simon Porte of Bedford came in on drums, Simon was working at 'The Music Centre' in Bedford town and was eager to have a go with us. Nigel Pegrum was, up until that time, the best studio drummer I had ever worked with. Simon seemed to be able to do just as well without thinking or worrying about it he just sat behind his kit puffing on a roll up, looking for all the world like he was basking on a summer's day. 'Sod the World' was his attitude and he delivered quickly and brilliantly.

Peter Lubbock joined us on bass, Ian Paul on trombone and Jay Alibone on tenor sax. We used the two horns in riff arrangements as opposed to soloing. Sax and trombone worked nicely together, on 'Just a Shaggy Dog Story', Rick Taylor played trombone with his pal Gordon Marshall on trumpet the effect of the trombone and trumpet while very good, was also very smooth. This would be Raunchier! Piece by piece it was turning into an album to be proud of.

The Masters were all completed and handed over to 'C.M'. in Yorkshire, the sleeve artwork completed and 'Rabble without a Cause' was released at the end of 1996/early 1997. The media received it well, the radio stations liked it and more importantly they played it. Reviewers, especially in the R& B field (I mean rhythm and blues, not rhythm and bass as is more recently known) loved it. Alan Pearce wrote in 'Blues Matters'; *"From the altogether intro of 'YOU LOSE' with Ben's gruff vocals and neat guitar work, you're in for a lively album. 'ALL I KNOW' in the right hands could be a chart record, it's that good.... 'YOU'LL NEVER KNOW' features Ben's best vocal and swings along..... 'TOLD BEFORE' brings the album to a close. I've heard good reports of this Bands live performance...try them!"*

The responses were very good but I had the impression I was a bit off the mark with regard to the style of the album. Afterwards I thought maybe we or I, had tried to be a bit too Bluesy, a bit too 'Back to Roots. Maybe the next one should be a bit more commercial, so we can get Radio Two and similar interest. RABBLE was a bit heavy for the Radio Two shows and similar stations. It has to be a balance, doing what you want to do and making it commercial enough for airplay.

I am happy with 'Rabble Without A Cause'. You just have to keep changing things and move along. It was done, we got the accolade, if not too many sales. It had however been 6 yrs since I had put anything out or had anything for sale, I thought 'next time we'll do better!'

Ruth and Dave Bulmer were trying hard with The Ben Markus Band and as we later became known – 'Markus'. Ruth did most of the telesales, people and by that she means Record shops, were just not in the mood to buy anything that was not from a massively known artist. I think things have changed a little for the better, especially were Live Music is concerned but it's not easy by any means to sell CD's to the main chain of record shops. But of course, nothing worthwhile ever is easy!!

One more 'Markus' would come into the world, 'BENJAMIN LEE MARKUS' was born in the new Bedford Sygnet Wing at South Wing Hospital on June 23rd 1997. We were told from the scans 3 months previously what gender he would be. The family sat in the Bedford Hospital Canteen and thought about names for him.
My father had been a Ben, I wasn't keen on this one being a Ben. I was always Benji until my father died but both girls and Sharon wanted him to be a 'Benji'. I was secretly very proud. So Benji it was. He is very similar to me in appearance, our baby photos are easy to mix up, (with the

small exception that mine are black and white and a bit crinkly now!)

*IS THERE A DOCTOR IN THE HOUSE?*
*(Yup, that's her in the Black gear playing the piano!)*

Sometimes I liked to change things, just because I like to change things. I thought about advertising for another female vocal, we could swap around with backing and widen the scope of the band. Placing an advert in the 'Loot', your friendly neighbourhood Freebie, I had a call from a woman called Stavia. A very unusual name and an exceptional woman. She said she had played keyboards/piano and wrote new material constantly, she also wanted to do some lead vocals. She'd never been in a Band but always wanted to be in one. Would we consider her? "Yea, too right, come on up and we'll discuss it".

All the other women who were responding to the add were not what I was after. Most were wanting to be a Spice Girl, one girl actually modelled her self on 'Baby Spice' and showed me photos of her 'Stage Outfit'. Her stage outfit.....Well....it was a couple of pieces of string that you could put it in your pocket, (when she sang you knew why she needed that outfit!)

Stavia Blunt was a consultant Neurologist at the Hammersmith Hospital. Very impressive but she could sing, play and her songs were pretty good as well. She turned up at Wilstead and wasn't at all what I was expecting. (She'd said she was a doctor and I really was expecting a mousy type of women who wanted to have a go at something different.)

Tall dark and attractive, she was dead keen to join. We began re-hearsing songs for a new album. I'd not yet got the full go ahead from 'Making Waves' (the label we actually signed to which is part of CM) but I felt pretty sure that would be a formality. (It was)

This time I wanted to use a recording studio in Northampton I had used a few times a year or so back.

THE LODGE NORTHAMPTON.

Max Read and Robert John Godfrey run the 'Lodge Recording Studios'. Robert John also founded 'The Enid', a Classical Rock outfit with a good pedigree known nationally. The studio was at the time about on par technically speaking, with EMI'S Abbey Rd 7 yrs previous, very good and more importantly, they knew how to get the best sounds from it. I felt we would come away with something special!

The material for MAGIC GARDEN would be an equal split of Stavia's and mine with Melanie writing her first real offering. She'd been writing in her room and asked if I could help her with a song and lay down some chords? The song was brilliant, much better than a first attempt had the right to be. 'Here With You' was many people's favourite track on 'Magic Garden'. So much so, it was re-produced on a later album and became one of that albums singles.

John Morrey from the early days of 'The Markus Band' after the families move back to Bedfordshire, excelled on bass. John is one of the best bassists I know, he can, when playing as a 3 piece, make his bass guitar sound very big. I wasn't 100% sure what he'd be like on recordings but I needn't have worried, he was Great!

Simon Porte was happy to join us again on drums. This collection of songs were going to be softer, it wasn't intended that way but with the changed line up, it started to sound a bit Fleetwood Mac-ish. I liked it! Melanie and Stavia got on great, we all did. It was a good album, Simon's laid back style however gave me a few grey hairs.

I try to organise studio time in a certain way, guide guitars first, guide vocals, proper guitars, keyboards, bass, drums in between keyboards and bass so forth and so on. Although it's best to get the bass and drums to record together if you can, desk space doesn't always allow it though.

Simon was due to lay down the drums for 4 tracks on the Thursday. He was due in at 11.am, it was now 12.30 and no sign of Mr Porte. Max nervously said more than once, "I hope he comes soon Ben, we have to finish at 5 today." "You and me both!!" I replied.

1pm and Simon was still not there, he didn't have a mobile either. About 1.45 he casually walked in, roll up wedged between his lips..."Al right Ben, how's you doin?"

I really thought, 'we'll never do all these tracks today' and Simon couldn't do any other day, it had to be today or not at all. Max said "Just not enough time Ben, you'll have to get someone else"

As Simon set up his drum kit, Max and his assistant were standing ready with mic stands ready to place around the drums before they were even set up, they truly looked like a pair about to take part in 60m hurdle race. This process alone takes 1-2 hours, it was now 3.30 and we had 4 tracks to do before 5pm.

Max played the tape, Simon had not even heard the songs, there had been no rehearsal of any kind but I didn't really want to tell Max this at the time. He started with 'TIRED' a 'rocky' offering from Stavia that would appear on the new album.

"Once through for listening", Simon said, "Roll the tape and record this one!"
He did it... perfectly! Time, style, emphasis, everything! "Shit! He's good." said Max. That put a smile back on my face. Simon did all the tracks equally as fast and he was packing up his drums by 4.45pm!!

This was also a very sad time on a personal level as our marriage had been having troubles and we decided objectively to separate. The children suffered a lot of pain for which I'm truly sorry. I hope we did things as easy and painless as it was possible to do considering the circumstances. Sharon and I are still friends to this day, I don't think anyone experiencing a similar situation can hope for more than that.

Chapter 10.

We had another album. 'MAGIC GARDEN' was 12 tracks long, some soft tracks, some raunchier ones and a reggae track another from the pen of Stavia that would be the designated single after Dave Bulmer said it was by far the best track on there. We had some nice string sounds courtesy of Max Read and a softer feel all the way around. 'Making Waves' didn't need too much prodding with 'Magic Garden but this time I wanted to have a bit more control and input over the artwork. I wasn't too impressed with the sleeve on 'Rabble Without A Cause', it was OK but it wasn't great.

Melanie and I took the trip to Harrogate, home of 'Making Waves', Ruth Bulmer was there for our entire visit and made us both feel very welcome. She and Mel chatted a lot as indeed Ruth and I did. Ruth is a lovely person, cheerful, intelligent, she was I think responsible for us being signed to the label. She kept telling her husband, "You'd better sign this lot"! Get their wives on your side, the husbands soon follow.

Andy Northing was 'Making Waves's' designer. We all sat around the computer throwing in ideas etc and we came away with what I thought was our best sleeve to date. You will all know from browsing through record shops, if something looks like it should be in the bargain bin, that's how you and everyone else will treat it. It's important to get to the right people with a sleeve, just putting pictures of the Band on the front is a tad over-used and a bit boring. I like to see more than that with creative photography or an illustration.

*LAST OF THE MOHICANS*

Also around this time, (Magic Garden) I'd changed my look. I'd had longish hair off and on for some years but it had thinned. I could still keep it long, sweeping it back but it was becoming a nightmare on stage with hair gel. One night when the venue was hot and I was hot, I started feeling the blue gel easing down my forehead with the sweat, "That's it, it's coming off!"

A few days later I'd cropped it down to a number 1, then went a stage further and shaved the lot off. I couldn't do the pretty boy look any more, well, to be honest I never could so the 'Mean' look would suit me fine. And, it was much cooler in venues with all the hair shaved off, occasionally I felt a bit chilly though. One day while I was sitting outside the Library in Luton by the Arndale, an incredibly attractive blonde woman just came over and started stoking my head!!! She then just kissed me on the head and walked off down the street, still flabbergasted, I called out to her "At least tell me your name?" I shouted. She just turned and sensuously blew a kiss from her hand! I wanted her name, if only to retell the story.....no one would believe that one!! That had NEVER happened to me with a full head of hair, I loved the 'Kojak' look!

'Magic Garden' was released New Year 1999. Stavia, who lived in the Putney area of London, started getting us lots of London Gigs. There are a hell of a lot of venues in London for Bands to play at. Trouble is, promoters expect the Bands to bring their own crowds. We're Bands, not promoters, its the promoters job to bring a crowd, that's all he has to do. So many Bands play usually for nothing in the Capital. We did start attracting crowds though, in the main thanks to Stavia and her contacts at the hospitals but we were playing very regularly at; 'The Half Moon' in Putney, 'The King's Head' in Fulham, 'The Red Eye Club', 'The West 14 Club'. The most prestigious of these London venues was 'The Rock Garden' in Covent Garden, it was a busy time for the band.

The 'Rock Garden' was situated on the north side of the Piazza, it was horrible to get to logistically on a Saturday though. The crowds there are very large throughout the day. Our first performance at the venue was a Saturday, Melanie and I pulled up in my old Astra Van which was loaded down with amplifiers at midday. We had to inch our way through the milling crowds, it was quite scary driving through a sea of people.

I backed up to the entranceway and I opened up the back door. Melanie had been directing me backward, one of the 'Mime Artists' was on duty, the 'silver man' with the bicycle. He'd been dead still for quite a while now, I simply forget to tell Melanie they were mime artists and NOT statues. Just as she approached him, she had been totally ignoring what she thought was a statue, he picked up the bike and did a 180 degree turn. He had realised Melanie was oblivious to him and was trying to get the maximum effect from his action. He got the effect!....Mel screamed at the top of her voice seeing this 'Statue' suddenly come to life! The crowd laughed, Mel was very embarrassed, she marched up to the 'Mime' and half heartedly pushed him just to get her own back but there was a smile on her face so I knew she had taken the incident in good spirit! She still remembers it though...

Steve 'Woody' Woodward again joined 'Markus' as we were now termed, for the slightly different sound we had on 'Magic Garden', this time on bass. Woody and I can play together for long periods, then we have a break and go do something else on our own. We've known each other since we were 11 yrs old, the friendship has lasted an incredible amount of time. He's more like my brother.

At the time of writing he's doing his own thing again as indeed I am with 'Markus' for the 'Time To Move On' album (A fantastic album on sale at your record store for the miserly price of £10.49.....get your copy today!!!) but we'll be playing together again before long if I know anything.

Steve Foggin was brought out of hibernation on drums as Simon Porte was busy putting together a band with his brother. So this 5 piece toured around the Capital. I had, as mentioned, an old Vauxhall Astra Van. Bit of a come down from the BMW 735 days. We would head off to London on a Friday or Sat night and Melanie usually managed to convince Woody that she should sit in the front and leave poor old Woody sitting in the back. "Oh ok Mel, I'll climb in the back" and he did Bless him. We would finish at the venues usually around midnight, load up and head for home. I have to admit I sweat a tad when I'm playing and singing, I always change my clothes afterward so I stay Minty fresh! But I usually need a fry up on the way home, I suppose it's due to the loss of salt. But we had some really good nights playing a gig, then three or more of the band sitting in a café or restaurant at 2am in the centre of London. Really good times!

'Magic Garden' did well with airplay and with the media. This time Anna Pukas of the 'Daily Express' wanted to do a piece, in the main about the Erstwhile Ms Blunt being a doctor and a 'Rock Chic' but the piece was very well written and balanced between Stavia's life and that of the Band.

We also attracted the interest of the German National Television. A programme called 'Blitz' followed Stavia around her hospital for the day then came to a gig we had that night at 'The Half Moon in Putney'. Melanie said, "I don't want to do any interviews" "Fair enough" I replied. I was more worried about having the place looking empty for the television cameras, we usually had a good turn out but we've also had nights when the bands could outnumber the audience.

It was a Friday night and 'The Half Moon' was the busiest I think I've ever seen it, I think it was a 'Capacity Crowd'. It seemed like standing room only. The cameras came up on stage, it is very

61

hard playing with a television camera two inches from you nose but you just have to ignore them. Afterwards, the reporter interviewed Stavia, myself and Steve Foggin. Mel said "Why didn't they want to interview me?"

I was fairly glad they didn't interview Woody though, during the sound check and rehearsal. He'd been using a Monty Python style of German accent for the intros.

"ZISS IS A SONG CALLED 'YOU LOSE' IT'S NOT ABOUT ZEE WAR.......BUT YOU DID'NT WIN!!!" "ZISS IS A SONG CALLED 'I DON'T NEED YOU' BUT IT IZ NOT THE FURHER SINGING TO MUSSOLINI!!"

That's all we needed, Woody getting us totally banned in Germany!!

'Magic Garden' is the album I see the most of around the country. People tell me they've seen it all over from the North to Devon and as far afield as Scotland. It has also sold the most since 'Shaggy Dog Story'.

Stavia now however wanted to branch out on her own, preferring to play a smooth jazz style than the type of music we where we were doing. Melanie's voice had been getting stronger and stronger, she was doing quite a few vocals on lead. I asked if she felt like taking over the tracks Stavia had been singing?

Melanie had in the past, been a bit sheepish at the microphone. Her voice was always there, strong and unique but I just don't think she believed she was that good, we would have to see how she did. She instantly said "yes" though.

Woody had other pastures to follow so Rob Butterfield auditioned and proved to be yet another great bass player and a good guy into the bargain. Stan Shepherd was now playing drums. Whether they find me or I find them I don't know but they've all been great over the years. (There were some 'Bad' ones but I'm not into Law suits and I got rid of them quickly anyhow!!)

Rob's a big guy, about 6'4", Stan about my height at 6'1", we certainly were one of the 'tallest' bands around. We rehearsed a new set, a bit rockier than we had been playing with Stavia and we again went out as 'THE MARKUS BAND'. I tend to use that name more for Rhythm and Blues

Band and 'MARKUS' for the Prog Rock/Funk line-ups.

One night we were playing at 'Zak's Place' in Wolverton Milton Keynes. For me it happened suddenly, Mel would probably remember it differently but she just blew the crowd away together with Rob and I. I can't explain it, she just moved it all into another gear. She was belting out 'Heart of Shame' from the 'Rabble' album like she was the only Diva on the planet. She held the mic stand up high in a way I've only seen Rod Stewart do and sang for all she was worth! I felt tears welling up in my eyes with pride.

In the early days when the promoters heard my daughter was one of the singers in the band, they sometimes wrongly assumed she was only there because she was my daughter. When they heard her sing, they then thought I was only there because I was her Dad!!!

*NEW BLOOD.*

Back to the LOOT!
I advertised for a keyboard/piano player, one night arriving home I found a decidedly strange message on my machine.

"This is Dean.....Dean Rees, I play a Hammond....a real Hammond, not the crappy keyboard type stuff. It's the real thing. I live in Milton Keynes, like to see what you're about.. Thank you very much!! This is Dean Rees!" the voice sounded like Max Wall.

I went around to Dean's house on a Sunday dinnertime with little Benjamin strapped into the back of the car in his car seat.   Dean was in his early twenties, hippy in style and totally into the type of Bands I'd listened to in my teens. His house was full of vinyl records, posters and he could really play the Hammond Organ. He plays it like I do a guitar, a soloing instrument. A lot of keyboard players tend to use their instrument as a background wash, a rhythm instrument purely for singing along too. Dean is more akin to Keith Emerson. He liked what we were doing and wanted to have a go.. It started to sound like 'Santana' meets 'E.L.P'. Everyone loved it!

*A HOUSE FULL OF GHOSTS!*

The line-up was now Rob, Dean, Stan, Melanie and myself.  We were scheduled to have a 4 way rehearsal at Peartree Bridge in Milton Keynes. Melanie couldn't make it but I can't remember why. We all pulled into the 'Interaction' facility in Milton Keynes, not so hot for acoustics but very cheap at £10 a night. Split that between 4-5 of you (I usually ended paying Mel's share) and it's great value  Tonight however it had been double booked, another band were there and as they were more keen to rehearse than our lot, (they had set up first) we had to defer.

We discussed what to do. "Let's go down the pub" said Dean (Like he's never said that phrase before!!) Follow me Chaps we got into our vehicles and drove towards Bedford. When Sharon and I separated she had stayed in the Wilstead house and I moved out, the girls had electing to come with me at that time. 46 Luton Road Wilstead had been scheduled for demolition and Sharon had moved out. There were plans for hundreds of houses on our old home site.  I helped her find another place and assisted with the move. The house was, I knew, totally empty.   I wonder....?
The convoy drove into the yard of 46 Luton Rd on an autumn night. "Shhhh, try and keep it down" I said not wanting to let neighbours hear, almost feeling like we were naughty boys. (Fat chance, we were about to let go with a combined 800 watts of guitar, Hammond and drums.....shhhing them was a little superfluous!!)

I still had a key to the front door, yup, no one around, do the lights work?  Yup, there was still power on at the mains.

We began setting up in the very long dinning room next to the kitchen.  "Bloody hell" said Dean, "you used to live here?"

It was an impressive house and there were mirrors everywhere. The designer/owners either knew how to make it look big or they were completely vain!

I almost wished we'd not gone there that night because it stated to feel so strange being in this empty house. Mel had more or less grown up there, Julia did too, Sean was just a toddler when we moved there and Benjamin Lee was born while we lived there. I could feel the Families history and past catching up with me but we played a good set, which was the last thing that ever occurred in 46 Luton Rd, Wilstead Bedfordshire. It was destroyed 3 days later, so it was a very fitting end for the place. However, I did take one last memory from it.

There was a door frame between the hall and the kitchen. ALL of my children's heights and dates were marked in pen on the frame, from a couple of feet all the way up to the 5'10" Melanie now stood in stocking feet. I just couldn't let this be demolished. I always carried my old Fire Axe around in the boot of my van. As the lads drove away, I watched them drive up the road, making sure they would not see my outburst of sentimentality. I got my old 'Axe' and sneaked back into the empty house. I broke away the support to the frame that enclosed a piece of my children's development and loaded it into the van. I still have the frame portion today. I turned the lights out and said good bye to the home we lived in for 10 years and drove out of the drive for the very last time. Christ I'm a soft Git!!

*STAN THE MAN*

Stan Shepherd, (his name actually wasn't Stan, but he never did tell me how it came to be Stan now) liked to live a bit on the dangerous side. He had a wife, he had a girlfriend, he'd had the girlfriend for 10years, had children with her he had the wife longer...I don't know how they never came to know each other....but they would. Stan's life turned upside-down and he had to pack it in for a while. So Rocket (real name Ron....can't drummers cope with the names their mothers give them? I didn't like Ben at first but I never swapped it for Hank or similar!!) Nice chap Ron, don't ever get in a car with him though. Rob learned this one night when Rocket offered to drive him to London, Rob's hair had been black before the trip, take a look at it now!!!

*THE TWO WORST THINGS IN LIFE!*

The girls and I had to move again. At first we'd moved into a friend's daughters house but that was short term, she was going to sell it so, we had to move again. We managed to get a nice place in Silsoe. There wasn't too much to move across, most of what we had in 'Flitwick' belonged to the house. It would be hard starting from scratch as we had very little. So I was on the scrounge for things second hand. Geoff gave me a fridge, "It's old Ben but it still works" It had sat in one of his offices he was then renting out. I picked it up the day we moved into Silsoe. Julia was in the old house, Melanie was at the new one and I kept going between the two, ferrying items across in the Astra van.

I bought the fridge in, it was a bit smelly and needed a clean. "Be a darling Mel, clean this out for me please?" She gave me a 'Melanie' look but agreed to doing the task. She was wearing my old Fire Service overalls, so not what most women would deem attractive I suppose. Just as she got to the point of being filthiest, I called her outside our new neighbour 'Nila' had come to say 'Hello' and I wanted her to meet my eldest daughter. I was totally ignorant of the fact Mel would've liked to look nicer (so that didn't put her in the greatest of moods...whooops. It got worse though). She'd made the old fridge look a treat, I plugged it in and turned on the mains. It began spitting, popping and then a small puff of smoke came out of the back and all the lights and fuses blew..."Whooops" I said trying to look flippant so as to unwind the situation. Mel raised one eyebrow 'Spock' fashion. "I'm filthy and I'm tired, you made me meet someone dressed like this" she said as she motioned to what she was wearing. "They say that children coping with divorce and moving are the 2 WORST things you have to deal with in life...so I'm having a FUCKING BAD DAY!" It was the only time I had ever heard Melanie use the 'F' word. On the next round trip I picked up Julia and bought Melanie the biggest bar of chocolate I could find!!

*CHALK AND CHEESE.*

As in every walk of life there are 'Good 'uns' and there are arseholes. The Music industry is no different. (After reading about the move and Melanie you'll probably think I'm in the last category.....I'm not I'm lovely!)
We were playing at the 'Roadmender' in Northampton's town centre backing a sixties/seventies band whose name shall remain unmentioned (but it's one syllable and begins with an 'M'.) I'm not knocking their music but they are a real shower on a personal basis. Before we played that night Dean had been a BIG fan, I had said during our chats that I had heard of them but in fact I hadn't really, I just didn't want to look a Pratt!.

They were assholey over where we put our gear, complaining to the management how long we were going to do and generally being a bunch of old bitter farts! We did the sound check and Melanie was totally on song. I think she scared them, she really can belt the songs out. None of this band were strong singers and this young lass had them all running scared.

During our set they pulled out the monitor speaker's wires (stage speakers that allow the Band to hear what they are doing) in a bid to disrupt our set but it didn't matter. Mel and the rest of us have played dozens, hundreds of times without monitors. We just do it, Rob watches the drummer, I watch Dean and we all stay aware of each other. But that was one Gig that we didn't go home that night on a high.

And then the other side of the coin, you meet a Gent. We were backing 'Medicine Head' and they were truly known, just about everyone I talked to knew them. Everyone who I told could remember 'One on one is one', (Medicine Head's biggest hit.) John Fiddler was the lead singer/guitarist/songwriter, he was great. He chatted at length when neither of us were playing and was full of praise for the 'sound' we had, the combination of guitar/Hammond/flute does make a unique sound. He even offered to take us all for meal afterwards, only Mel and I had the time though.

I'd had a rough time during that particular day. I had a funeral to attend. I've attended a lot of funerals but I've never gotten used to them and I hope I never do. Tony Holloway was one of my ex Station Officers at Luton Fire Station, to say everyone liked him sounds clichéd and over used, so I shall tell you what type of man he really was.

I was a fairly new driver on the main appliances. We were at a field fire down a very tight lane in the Farley Hill area of town. Tony asked me if I could get the Water tender Ladder down the lane. "Yea....no bother" came the Cocky reply. I drove the pump down there fairly easy, the crews put the fire out and I reversed the Appliance back out again. We stopped to load up the hoses we'd used, Tony beckoned me to the side of the 3 week old Ford Appliance.

"Yea...what's up Guv?" He pointed to the side of the pump.... AGGGGGH!!!
It was covered in scratches, not deep but hundreds of them. It looked a right mess, I was the youngest driver and A.D.O. 'Dolly' Gray would kill me, or worse, take me off driving! "It's al right" Tony said, "I'll put down I was driving the pump on the accident report form...I don't give a Toss if they stop me driving" Most officers wouldn't do that, if they did, most officers would then tell everyone else about it, just to take the Piss. Tony Holloway never told a soul and he never even mentioned it to me again, in fun or otherwise.

Today of all days I had to attend his funeral. Normally on the day of a Gig I would not have gone but I just had to attend for Assistant Divisional Officer Holloway. Not only was he a Gent, he played guitar and drove a motorcycle and continued to do so literally just months before he died young of Cancer.

What has this got to do with the 'Medicine Head' gig? When John Fiddler heard the story of Tony Holloway, what type of Fireman he was and his love of guitars, he did a special rendition of John

Lennon's 'Working Class Hero' and dedicated it to Tony Holloway!

*AND YET MORE NEW BLOOD*

Rocket was a good drummer but he was not happy playing the wider based styles and material we were doing. So back to the LOOT! This time Karl Randall answered, we met over my place. He had trouble finding my house in Silsoe, he's known me nearly 5 years and he still has trouble finding my house in Silsoe. He has trouble finding venues too but he's one of my closest friends and probably THE best drummer I've ever used.

Karl is the same age as Dean Rees, they like the same types of music, they dress pretty similar so I thought those two would hit it off. They did. The night Karl turned up to play I was a bit late for rehearsal, Rob and Karl had run through a few things and Rob came outside to meet me as I began unloading my gear. "He's bloody good, where'd you find him?" Thank you LOOT.

*ODDS AND SODS.*

This line up was now pretty stable, we gigged extensively for a couple of years. London when we could, all over the Home Counties, we all got on well. All the band have looked on Melanie more like a niece than a band member. They always watched out for her at gigs. It was a 'real' good atmosphere.

We played in some quite diverse places as well. One night at 'The Edge' in Park St Luton, it was filled with teenagers from the University. Melanie was older than most of the audience. I thought we were going to bomb but we didn't. We kept it a bit heavier than usual, more overdrive on the guitar and Dean gave the Hammond more welly but we went down unexpectedly well. It was bloody loud though, one of the only times I HAD to use earplugs!

Being able to adapt to the crowd or a situation is something we are good at. Another night in St Albans we were playing 'The Horn Reborn'. Dean couldn't make it so I had managed to get a friend to ask his friend. 'Zach Barrett' to come along on tenor sax. It was a pleasure playing with him. We all changed our style and played much jazzier that night. Karl called his missus "Carolyne, can you get over here tonight, we've got a great saxophonist, he just turned up out of the blue", which wasn't totally untrue. Zak could solo without taking a breath for what seemed like an eternity. He told me after he'd learned the circular breathing technique. His scales and lines were nothing short of brilliant, we just sang the verses and let him have his head with the soloing, it worked like a dream.

One sore point I know Melanie would want me to mention somewhere is her frustration at my, shall we say, occasionally forgetting lyrics. This never happens on 'Covers', just my songs, (I wrote the lyrics I can sing what I bloody well like unless of course someone is harmonising with me). Melanie will often harmonise behind the main vocal, it does sound great the way she does it, sometimes directly in synch with me, sometimes she purposefully delays it a half beat. This is hard however but it gets even harder when the person your singing with forgets the 2nd verse and repeats the 1st one or sings the 3rd verse twice!! One such night in London BOTH our microphones were up loud. We were performing I think 'Running' from the Magic Garden album. I could not for the life of me remember the first line of the second verse......so I sang the third verse......The look I received from my daughter told me she wasn't very amused. She didn't say too much afterwards but that look can kill!.....or at least hurt a lot......especially if it becomes infected!!

Chapter 11.

This is another of those Chapters that 'could' be labelled a bit boy-ish. The sound the band was now making was quite unique, it comes a lot from having the Hammond Organ and guitar acting like a backwash underpinning the drums and bass. Dean and I will then trade off soloing as and when required, and the horns or flute will have their own space and perform a sub melody that augments the vocal line.

As I had my passion chapter about guitars, I wanted Dean to have his say about his.

We sat in the Railway Swan (stupid name for a pub) in Woburn Sands one night for the usual 'update' meeting.....(yes it was a ploy for us all to go out and have a drink!). I told Dean I was working on the book and wanted some history about Hammond Organs, where they came from? Why? Etc etc. All the following was written down on beer mats so if there are some errors, sorry.

The Hammond Organ Company of Chicago has been around since Adam was a lad! Truly. They began, I believe, making their product in the early decades of the 1900's. They had originally been made with the intention of selling them to Churches where a full blown organ was not appropriate. They were for the time, the ideal 'portable' substitute. (After carrying this monstrosity around with Dean Rees I would NEVER, EVER call a Hammond Organ 'Portable'!!)

Two early pioneers of the Hammond were Jimmy Smith and Jimmy McGriff. These musicians were playing music in a Jazz/Blues idiom and were probably among the first to use a Hammond in a contemporary setting. In the UK I think one of the first would have been 'Alan Price' with 'The Animals' and 'Georgie Fame', who along with the Blue Flames, had many 'Hit Records' in the sixties.

Dean Rees is very touchy if anyone calls his Hammond a keyboard. Which of course it isn't. Keyboards began to dominate modern music in the 80's using digital technology, Yamaha are probably the best known but we've all seen and heard what is around these days. (Whenever I think of 'Keyboards' , I get an image of 'Mel Smith' closing the programme of the 'Smith & Jones' show with his sequin jacket and frilly shirt!). The Hammond however makes it's noise by mechanical means. Looking inside one, it resembles the workings of a clock, an old wind up type. Spindles and wheels can be clearly seen and it works by magnetic contacts i.e. a motor power generator running tone wheels.

I have used keyboard players who play Yamaha DX7's and similar but Dean swears, and I fully back him on this, they do not come close to a 'Real Hammond' sound. Trouble is, as I said earlier, it weighs a Damn ton!

Dean has a system for moving it now, unloading it from his van he has a wheeled trolley assembly to make things a bit easier but there have been quite a few times it has still needed the whole band to help get it up a stairway, or down a basement. We used to have a regular spot at the 'Rock Garden' in Covent Garden as mentioned but there is just NO WAY all of us could manoeuvre the Hammond down this twisty basement venue.

The Hammond took a bit of stick in recent years thanks to the BBC series 'Red Dwarf', the Geeky 'Rimmer' enjoying albums such as 'Reggie Wilson plays Funking up Wagner' supposedly performed on a 'Hammond' but despite this slander the instrument has long been 'Cool'.

After the Georgie Fame days, Keith Emerson made it BIG first with 'The Nice', then later E.L.P. (Emerson, Lake and Palmer). Listen to many Progressive Rock tracks, as likely as not you will hear a Hammond in the production. It blends with Rock music like no other keyboard type instrument, piano included.

Dean plays it like a soloing instrument, he can do the backwash type of rhythm but see him in the middle of a solo and it's fantastic, all integral to the appeal of the Hammond. The instrument looks, as well as sounds good.

There were many models, 'Model A', then the 'BC' throughout the 40's and 50's. 'C3'S' 'B3's. 'A100's'. Dean now uses as his 'Best' model, an M100 (but with same pre-amp as B3, this I'm told makes a difference, all I know is it sounds 'huge').

We had a close call one night with Dean's Hammond, the Medicine Head Gig (mentioned elsewhere in the book). Dean's brother in law Stuart comes to many gigs, he'd had a few one night and kept coming over to Dean while he played. (Dean usually sets up on the floor of this particular venue, there was a shortage of space on the stage and it was hard to lift the big Organ up there anyway) Stuart inadvertently knocked over Dean's pint of Guinness, the drink went all over the keyboard area, into the switches, everywhere. Suddenly the Hammond died!.... We all thought it was going to be its last swell of noise but Dean shut off the switches quickly in a bid to save his beloved instrument. Waiting a few seconds he clicked it back on, there was a very very strange sound, like a fairground ride organ coming back to life after a long time in hibernation when the sound slowly got back to pitch, luckily it was ok. Dean was looking a tad sheepish but he winked back at me when the original tone came back on line.

At another venue in Buckinghamshire, the place was a bit short of space with no proper stage. So they slotted the Hammond in between a couple of Pinball machines just around the corner away from the main bar area, I never saw him for the rest of the night....could still hear him though!...

Chapter 12.

*THE EXILE FROM NEW JERSEY*

If you don't go backward, or standstill, then the only way to go is forward. This sounds silly and non-nonsensical but it is true. Bands have to be constantly changing and adapting to situations, the Beatles did this admirably. Listen to 'She Loves You' and 'I am the Walrus' back to back, they sound like they were recordings from two different Bands. I have always tried to make sure things were growing, both in approach regarding how we get our stuff out to the media and the production of the albums.

But I was short of money, I couldn't afford to record another new album but I had to do something. So the only thing I could do, was to give some tracks a 'Facelift and see if we could get that out as another album. I re-mastered a few previous tracks, re-recorded some of the vocals on a few more. Melanie took over some tracks that Stavia had done on some 'Magic Garden' songs and we had 'New Jersey Exile' mastered and ready to go.

One of the tracks that I knew could be better was the original recording of 'Angelene' from 'Just A Shaggy Dog Story'. Due to the sheer amount of tracks used on the multi tape and the number of instruments on it, Nigel Pegrum's studio though good, was probably lacking a little bit in the mixing capabilities. Talking with Nick Webb from the Abbey Road Studios in north London. He said "Leave it with me"

A few days later he came back, one of his friends, Darren Godwin would have a go with 'Angelene' and see what he could do. FANTASTIC! Gonna do some recording at Abbey Road, the seat of power for 'The Beatles' and many more afterwards!

The producers at the studio I am told, can use the facilities for their own projects when they're not working. Darren offered to do some more recording and mix 'Angelene' to a standard we could use for a single. I went in to London one Sunday night at around 6pm. We worked through the night finishing about 9 the following morning it was a long busy night but we probably had just made the best track for 'New Jersey Exile. Darren thought he could make the intro more powerful so he played around with bits and pieces and ended up getting me to hit a power chord on the Gibson, then played it backwards. This gave the effect of the track starting from nothing and building up to

73

the huge power chord, it was impressive. The vocals were re-recorded and we changed the 'Hook Line', the lyrics in the chorus were now dominated by the words 'Over Now', so the song title was changed accordingly.

The horns originally performed by Rick Taylor in Newcastle were now big in the mix, as were the backing vocals. It had an expensive sounding sort of covering, or sheen to the production and I was very pleased as I left the St John's Wood building and made my way to the underground carrying the 'masters'.

This album was an odds and sods collection, it wasn't going to be ground breaking but I'm happy with it. Rob Butterfield, wanting to break into the Record Label Industry, offered to take it on for his own Blue Juice Label.

Again we achieved some very worthwhile airplay. The Daily Express did a full page feature on the album, my background and how I'd arrived at this point in time etc etc. 'New Jersey Exile' was due for release Spring 2001. When the 'Express' article appeared but there were problems in manufacture so the release was delayed for about another month. The headline that appeared in the Daily Express read – 'HEAR SAY ARE AN INSTANT BUT I'M STILL TRYING AFTER 30 YEARS.' Christ, have I really been at this 30 years, God that makes me sound old... Anna Pukas did a very nice article, no jibes, no misquotes, it was all as I had relayed to her 3 days earlier. Thanks Anna, there is integrity in the national papers.

The 'Trisha' programme called and wanted me to join one of her shows. "What's the basis of the show?" I asked the researcher. "How the music industry and Show business can screw your life up" she replied. "Music hasn't screwed my life up" I replied. "You must feel bitter you've not made a fortune by now" she countered. "No" I replied. "Oh" she said. "Sorry to bother you" "that's ok", I said "the phone was ringing anyway!!"

We could all do with a bit more cash, everyone but we only spend it when we have it. I've been lucky over the past 20 yrs because I have been doing what I wanted to do, what I always knew I should be doing, I'm happy. There are a lot of things I could change with hindsight but I didn't have hindsight when I made the initial decisions. If me auntie had balls etc etc.

It is possible to do ok and NOT be mega famous, probably better if you're not. I can walk down the street and no one bothers me. (With the exception of the Sodding Banks!!) I always have another gig to look forward to, there's always the next album, or song to write, it's great! The press and the music media have always to a man or review, been fair with me. I think the way and the only way to do this is to totally detach yourself from any end result. If you're doing it for fame, forget it, you won't achieve anything due to being tied to an 'end result'. If you truly enjoy playing recording, whatever, then do it. That goes for acting, writing dancing, anything you feel is the path for you. Give up your job and go do it, you won't regret it. (Having your wife or partner hit you over the head with a bat may make regret a teensy bit more evident when she cannot afford to pay for food....in other words talk with her or him first) But if you have unfulfilled aspirations I know from the experience of watching those around, this can kill you quicker than anything!

I'd still recommend anyone trying to make it in music or similar not to but if I can put you off, you shouldn't be doing it anyway!

Thus endeth the lesson!!

*THE FEMALE ELVIS!!!*

Melanie was getting near to leaving school and wanted to do something with her qualifications. She had her A levels but she was a bit lost with regard to what she wanted to do. When I first left the Fire Service I did look into a few things, one was radiography. Sharon and I had a few discussions with her on what was available in the job market. She seemed to like the idea of being a Radiographer. After going through all the channels Melanie applied and was accepted at University for a BSc Radiography course, she carried on with the Band when she could but she did want me to find someone else to replace her, for while at any rate.

I started advertising again. Lisa Rocco called me. She certainly had a good telephone voice and she'd done some Band work. She had a cheeky nature and was very enthusiastic. I said I would go down to London to meet her as she was going to be late home from work that evening and I had nothing to do that night.

Lisa was a very attractive sultry woman in her thirties. Of Italian decent, she was a full time hair stylist and a make up artist. She was also very streetwise. She auditioned and got on well with the lads having learned what I'd asked her to learn for the first rehearsal and she did sing the songs very well. So we were off and running again. Her first Gig was at 'The Horn Reborn' no nerve problems manifested themselves, she was good.

## BIG GEORGE WEBLEY

Big George Webley is a DJ on BBC Radio Bedfordshire, he also writes articles for magazines and I believe is a bass player as well. He wanted to do an interview on air for the release of 'New Jersey Exile'. Lisa offered to come along as a new member of the Band and put her two cents worth in. We did the usual Interview type of stuff, where to get the album, he played some songs. Then George asked Lisa what bands she'd been in. It transpired that Lisa had been an 'Elvis Impersonator', she'd not told me this....she told 'Big George' though. That was it, George wouldn't let her go until she had performed an Elvis piece. Never tell a DJ something like that...You'll live to regret it...it's on tape and it will last forever.

Lisa stayed a while but we really needed to replace the instrument we'd lost with Melanie's flute. Rebecca Gibson then called me as she'd recently moved into the area (after yet another add in the LOOT) and was looking for Band work to supplement her teaching profession on saxophone. She had a real raunchy style on sax, could also play flute and quickly slotted into the Band. Plus, she could sing, differently to Melanie and Lisa but a damn good voice all the same.

Horn players tend to take on loads of work and sometimes spread themselves thinly, so we also had the benefit of Vicky Cowles around this time. It usually worked well, if Rebecca were busy, Vicky would usually be around and vice versa, we always seemed to cover the Gigs somehow.

Many people over the last few years have asked me why we don't push our stuff to the major record labels any more? Basically, I don't want to. It's a combination of they're wrong for us and they wouldn't be interested in us if we did.

Major Record labels are not really about music any more. They're about money (My favourite topic) and they are about committees. In 1983 when we did the first 'Nocturn Gate' LP, the cost of the disc was around 80p to produce and it had a retail of approx £4.00. With everyone taking a cut, you can more or less see who made what. The composers always have their fee set by the P.R.S. at 6.8% of retail, producers varied but were in the region of 5% if the producer was an executive producer – i.e. they were paying for the recordings.

Bands signed for a variety of percent's. I know the Beatles in later year managed to get 25% of retail out of EMI. I suspect the Prog Bands of the previous years got a little less. Then along came the Kylie/Jason type of act, I had a whisper from someone in the heart of 'Stock, Aitken & Waterman' that they were signed for two and a half percent of retail. I know a small portion of something big makes it worthwhile but this was more about control. With the artists getting those types of percent, they would be controlling very little of what went down onto tape.

There are always the big Indy Bands that will get through the Oasis's etc but the major Record companies really don't like them doing so. They'd rather have units they can control easier. Today the cost of CD manufacture is less than 50p per unit, I can get it done for that price, you know damn well the major's are probably paying 25p for each CD made, with a retail price of around £12 –14 now, the extra profit is going somewhere. The artists aren't getting it but some one is. So for us, the major label thing would just never happen. We get by.

*TREADING WATER*

At the end of 2002 Karl and Dean would get an offer to join 'Greg Ridley's Humble Pie'. Dean had some contacts in this area, he was friends with Steve Marriots widow Pat, he moved in those circles and often got gigs with the likes of Kenny Jones, Peter Frampton and other ex members of 'Humble Pie'. I'd have to more or less start from scratch with another line up. Rob stayed, Woody came back to play for the umpteenth time, we had Caddy Lee then Wayne Breed on drums. Vicky Cowles stayed around did quite a few gigs, Rebecca was always around if Vicky couldn't do them. I have to admit the majority of these gigs were in the dreaded £200 pub bands bracket. It didn't do a lot for the confidence but you just keep going, you have to...something will turn up, if it doesn't you have to make it turn up!

Chapter 13

In the summer of 2002 I met Isabel, a mutual friend had given her my number. Isabel had been writing lyrics and verses for years, always wanting to go further with them, not really sure how to but song writing or lyric writing was I think, how she always intended her work to be displayed.

Meeting in a Woburn pub we did get on instantly and formed a relationship that has had its ups and downs over a period of time. Sometimes its harder to match up your lifestyles than pure compatibility on a personal level. Anyway, to cut along story short, we write good songs together. We began writing them more or less right away. The very first of these was titled 'Got to Get Around You'. Isabel had the lyric for this and bought it for me to put music to. I usually do not like writing this way, much preferring to complete the music then, have a lyric put to the music, however this time it worked. The lyrics had to be cut and edited quite a lot but eventually it fitted very nicely.

I began putting these new originals into the set list of The Markus Band. The lads always seemed to like them, (they probably wouldn't say anything if they didn't though). Melanie had been through her University years and was coming back home. She'd been courting for a couple of years and her relationship was strong with Ric. She hinted a few times she might like to do a few gigs again, just a few to begin with. She came back for 'The Entertainment Shed' in Bedford. Quite a nice venue in the old part of Bedford along the Castle Road, very near to where Ronnie Barker was born. The Entertainment Shed was part of and attached to – The Gordon Arms. They've had some biggish names over the years and the place is better than a lot of the Music Pubs, certainly the best in Bedford.

Ms Fulcher and I would continue writing songs, I would still write on my own but we did a lot of good stuff together. Most of which would start with me writing a rough backing with an acoustic guitar on to a tape, humming or singing a possible melody line, then in this early stage of the song, let Isabel listen and see what type of lyric will be appropriate. I do find lyric writing a bit of a strain, often just rushing it and then getting disappointed so I leave the track. I like to write some songs that are NOT about relationships, political, historical, anything but relationship songs seem to be easier for me.

I know this is basically what Blues songs are about but I always liked it when Bands and artists wrote a non-love lyric. I guess love is just what dominates most peoples lives, so it's like a universally accepted common ground.

Melanie and I wrote a few songs when she had time in her busy University schedule, far and away the best of these was 'Don't Tell Me' A slowish song that had what I term a 'Waltz' rhythm to it. (Karl tells me it's not a Waltz but a
6-8 pattern.  I still say it's a Waltz!) 'City' another offering from Melanie and I. This song is about Luton, I always wanted to write a song about Luton, there's a lot you can write about Luton. (Technically not a city, Luton is much bigger than most Cities in this area) but the title City suited Luton and the song.

The songs were piling up over a year or more, they were good lyrics and crowds warmed to them.

It is very hard to play a new song to A, the band and B, audiences.  When I give the Band a blast with a rough lyric, I'll watch expressions to see what they really think as opposed to what they say. Most of the new songs seemed to get a good response, the one's that didn't, I ditched.

I know this might sound strange but for me song writing is quite an intimate affair, I don't feel comfortable song writing with another male. Maybe it's because it is a display of emotion that has to be shared and I can only do that in front of another woman with any degree of comfort. I think this may originally stem from my days in the Fire Service.

Things have changed in the past few years in the Service, counselling is available to crews that need it. I think it was available in the 70s' but had any crew asked for it, they would have at best, received an awful lot of stick and at worse, been regarded as 'Totally Soft' by colleagues. So you shut up. Every death and injury you see you try and play it down, make jokes about it after. (Obviously not in front of someone who is injured or their relatives, we weren't insensitive clods) This is a wrong frame of mind that I believe is disappearing from the Fire Service but it has left its mark on me.

More than once Band members have asked if they can write songs with me and I've usually found an excuse. I once heard Eric Clapton, I think it was a South Bank Show interview telling how when he's written a song it's like tearing your insides out and putting them on display. That's it exactly! So I prefer to write alone or with a female who I am emotionally close to.

79

I didn't know how or when I would try to make another album but things were heading that way. The Markus Band line up was not really keen to take on this commitment. That particular gang do it for pleasure but more akin to a hobby. They had very good jobs and would never want to leave them. As you may have gathered from these pages, it's more a 'Life' thing for me. With many of the pub gigs you
are playing to people who basically do not want you there. The pub pays your fee, the customers are NOT charged at the door. The idea is just to bring in custom. Many of the customers however just want to go there and drink, or talk with mates. So in some cases you're just in their way. They start talking louder and louder until they start to shout louder than the drums. Sort of a 'You're not stopping me doing what I want to do' attitude. Whereas music venues and the ones I term the 'Proper Music Pubs' have long-standing traditions of Good Bands so the people go there specifically to hear music. Cover's bands (Bands who play other artists or Hit songs) do not as a rule, go down well in the Proper Music Pubs. Whereas the opposite is true of the High St Pub night. If you don't play 'Covers' the crowds get agitated and start bellowing for 'House of the Rising Sun and this is where the divide is. I wanted more and more to play music venues with a set list that contained a majority of my or original songs.

So....something had to give. I was getting more browned off with playing in Bedfordshire Pubs, to the point I truly was thinking of stopping altogether.
I've thought many times about going to try my luck in America. I don't have to worry about work visas, I still have rights to an American Passport. I would however miss the children terribly though so that one is still on a back burner. Germany I'm told is an attractive possibility, I have sold many records there but whatever I did all I knew was the local pub scene was getting to me. However, in the summer of 2003 I realised it was going to be 20 yrs since the release of 'Nocturn Gate, we'll have to do something for that I thought!

*IT WAS 20 YEARS AGO TODAY!*

In the spring I arranged with 'The Woughton Centre in Milton Keynes for a Sunday gig to celebrate the 20 years since I first began serious recording. I wrote to just about everyone I had played with, either on record or live over that period of time. The list was huge;

Nigel Pegrum, Vince Cross, Mark Williamson, Steve Woodward. Alan Mickleborough, Rob Butterfield, Keith Green, Stan Shepherd, Rick Taylor, Julie Costello, Alison Sumner, Rebecca

Gibson, Vicky Cowles, Steve Foggin, Rupert Cook, Peter Lubbock, Ian Paul, Jay Alibone, the list really goes on and on. Of course Melanie was centre stage on vocals and for the first time, Julia Markus joined us on backing vocals.

Julia Markus has a gorgeous voice, but she doesn't seem to be too interested in doing singing at the moment. I don't push them (Melanie would probably disagree at this point but it's my recollections here). Before her diabetes she was beginning to do very well on the guitar. She was picking out quite complicated instrumental tunes such as 'Wipe Out' and few Shadows numbers when her diabetes was diagnosed. She stopped playing because she has to prick her fingers two and three times a day for the blood sample. She has to do this with her right hand and prick the fingers on her left, these are the fingers used on the fret board of a guitar. Her fingers were always sore and it just hurt too much to play any more, Julia always did seem to get the crappy end of the lollipop.

June 8th 2003 was the date, it was a Sunday dinnertime and free admittance.
A lovely big stage but then it needed to be, while not everyone could make it. There was no shortage of muso's. At any one time there was always 12 or more on stage. Some nice photos of the day were taken by Isabel. I had some of these made up into small display frames and I'm very proud to say, whenever I go around to band member's houses who are on that photo, the photos are mounted in very obvious places. (Either that or they hide them until I come around, bring them out for the visit and then hide them when I've gone!). The members who played that day were; *Myself, Melanie Markus, Julia Markus, Steve 'Woody' Woodward, Dean Rees, Karl Randall, Rob Butterfield, Alan 'Milky' Mickleborough, Rick George, Vicky Cowles, Wayne Breed. (I think that's the lot!)*

*'TIME TO MOVE ON'*

Thinking about making another album I contacted a few people who were left in record companies who I still knew. The number was dwindling. I won't give any names here but I was talking with a London label manager, I couldn't believe most of the conversation, this disbelief resulted in my writing to the Daily Mail, they published the letter and a BIG photo of the Band to go with it.

*"No one I know is happy with the state of contemporary music. At gigs, audiences hang around to see my Band afterwards to bemoan the situation with the multitude of 'Pop Idol' type programmes seemingly dominating the way forward with a guaranteed 'How to crack the Music Business'. The*

*fact that these programmes are so popular stems from a misconception; the voice while important, is not what it's all about.*

*For me Led Zeppelin were the biggest thing in the late sixties and early seventies. Anyone who argued that Jimmy Page, John Bonham and John Paul Jones were not as important as Robert Plant would be ridiculed. Ringo Starr has suffered many adverse comments over the years, with claims that his drumming wasn't very good. I know of no other drummer who could have made 'GET BACK' the unique (and to me, best) song it still is today. John Lennon, Sir Paul McCartney and George Harrison would agree I'm sure*

*Last week while talking to a 'record company' executive, trying to get him to see why he should have a go with our new album, I said "It really will cost you a fraction of what you spend on most artists because we play and arrange everything ourselves. He countered "Yea I know, but we only have to download a drum track from the Internet, put a couple of passing muso's on, tie in the voice of our latest 'big thing' – and BANG!" That said it all....*

The above appeared in the Daily Mail Wed 4th Feb 2004.

Chapter 14

I was now thinking quite seriously about how to get this new album off the ground. Then, what to do with it once it was recorded. I went to see Robert John Godfrey and Max Read to see what sort of price they would let me have 'The Lodge' for. Their prices are fantastic in this day and age, they are now completely digital. The old Studer A 820 24 track sits in the corner but they hardly ever use it any more, its prime use is for re-mixing customers old recordings and they still offer the studio with all the gear for £200 per 10 hour day. I'm not touting for business for them but this is astounding in 2004, I was paying more for Spaceward in 1983.

Now who to record with. I approached just about everyone I was using or had been using in the past few years. Karl Randall and Dean Rees had both come along to the 20th Anniversary gig and had enjoyed playing with me. They'd suffered a sad time when Greg Ridley had died quite suddenly of cancer, they were both gutted and spent a lot of time with Greg's widow. Greg Ridley was only in his fifties when he died.

So after sounding everyone out, I asked Karl and Dean to join me for a drink/discussion in the Swan Public House in Woburn Sands. Isabel came too as she was directly involved with her song writing and was turning out to be a very good radio promoter.

In a bid to boost some interest with 'New Jersey Exile, Isabel readily agreed to take a single or two around the radio stations. She had her BBC 'Pluggers' pass and started meeting with the various producers in Western House. Melanie's and my 'Here With You', the single she had the most success with. She was getting on great, especially with Colin Martin who is the Music Boss at Radio Two. His assistant Sue Kerridge was always helpful and encouraging as indeed the majority of the Western House producers are.

Trouble is the Radio Two play-list is very small, usually the domain of much bigger artists but smaller ones have and do make it onto the play-list, you just need the right song, at the right time with the right producers liking it. Sounds simple? well....maybe it doesn't!

I was expecting to do a lot of 'selling' to the 'Lads' because I was going to offer to do this new album as a sort of co-operative venture and that meant getting dosh out of their pockets so I put it to them.

"Right, how would you two like to join me and make a new album from scratch? New songs, everything. Just one problem. I'll have to ask you for a fairly big lump of money?"

"Fine by me" said Karl, "me too" said Dean. "I was expecting you two to be a bit quicker off the mark than that!!!"

We began meeting every week or so to discuss plans, what we would do with the finished recordings and how best to get an album made and in the shops. There's a huge amount of detail to finalise with an album, much of it non-music related but it all has to be done. Sending copies to Newspaper, magazines, promoters, radio stations alone accounts for approx 200 copies. There are hundreds of people you have to badger with it, just to get an ounce of publicity, which is the only way to get your albums across.

I knew of a few record labels I could approach with the finished product but they were more or less in the small league. I said in 1992 that I would never do another album on my own label. At the time I really meant it, I was now thinking to the contrary.

I had learned so much in the 12 yrs since the 'Supertrack' fiasco, I knew I could do at least as good a job as most of the smaller labels. With what I lack in finance, I can make up for with sheer hard work and knowledge of the industry.

I put it to the 'Lads' about an own label thing, expecting some resistance on this point but again I was wrong. "Yea, whatever you think is best Ben" was the unanimous response.

Right, it's settled.

### TIME TO MOVE ON

We began rehearsing the new collection of songs, originally intended to be called 'Out In The Cold' in March 2004, one of the songs having the same name. I had an old picture of I think, Shackleton, an Arctic explorer. I thought it would make a good sleeve, I could either super-impose our face shots inside the parkas of Shackleton and his men or just use the photo as it was. It was OK but OK sometimes just isn't enough.

84

When things are a bit quiet with live and recorded work, I do a volunteer portering job at Bedford South Wing Hospital. Melanie works there and sometimes it's my only chance to have a meal with her at dinner time in the hospital canteen. When I joined I thought I'd be pushing young nubile ladies around in wheelchairs, anyone who works in a hospital environment knows this just ain't true.

The types of patients who need portering are usually very ill, usually very old and usually very infirm but it's worthwhile, I work mainly with the ambulance crews. I was one of the only volunteers in that dept. If a volunteer is not there to bring down patients to the vehicles, ambulance crews have to leave their appliance, go to the wards and bring down the patients themselves. This can mean 15-20 mins (sometimes even half an hour or more) that they are NOT with their vehicle. These vehicles also stand-by for the emergency crews. They are what they term, H.D.U or High Dependency Units, so it's possible an ambulance could be 'Off the Run' because the crew are up on the ward getting a patient. This means an situation could come about where someone in the street in an emergency situation might not be seen quickly enough.

The Bedford bunch are a great team and I liked working with them, usually just one day a week. Roger Judd is the Supervisor at Sth Wing, he's also a BIG music buff. He started coming to Gigs virtually from the off and usually gets a good crowd when we play at a Bedford venue.

One Monday I was in an area of the hospital where, not to put too fine a point on it, the older patients are put when there isn't too much hope for them. In the main they are very ill and cannot look after themselves in any circumstance, they are in fact, put there to die.

As I was wheeling a patient out of one of the small side wards I noticed on the wall a striking illustration, mostly in blues and turquoises, the work was entitled
'Time To Move On'. Reading further I saw it was drawn by 'Toni' in 1995 and
the illustration was given to the ward for their kindness in looking after Toni's grandmother who had died in that year.

I loved the picture right away. As I wheeled my patient to her waiting ambulance I was thinking 'That'd make a brilliant sleeve, I must see if I can use it for the next album. Sod it! Use it for this one. You don't know if there will be another one' I told myself.

I sat thinking about who to ask. I asked Roger, who said try Monica his direct head and liaison with the hospital, she asked her head and so forth and so on. In the end I was speaking to the Head of the hospital Mr Morgan who said it was really down to the Sister of the Ward.

When a person donates something to a ward, it is then the property of that ward. The Sister is the legal boss of that Ward so she has the say. During my dinner break I went to see the Sister. She was fascinated by my request and instantly agreed to my taking the illustration and having it scanned. I took it that night and had it scanned within a few days. It was back on the wall in the John Bunyan Ward in Sth Wing with in one week and I had my sleeve cover.

The title 'Time To Move On' conjured up so much for me in many aspects of life. It was drawn with death in mind but it's so apt on a personal relationship level, well any sort of level really. I had a track that I wasn't sure what to do with, I knew it could be good but I needed something with a Hook to get it started. The phrase 'Time To Move On' just fitted the track like a glove. The song had originally been a soft Blues, almost a soft Jazz feel but a reggae beat fitted it much better now that the lyrics were taking shape.

Many times I have struggled with a song, it seems to start well, and then you get bogged down, either with the melody or usually for me, with the lyric. Then the sun shines and everything falls into place more or less instantly. 'Time To Move On' was one of the latter once I had the title.

We were getting to a point where I was happy to make a start in the studio. I don't like over rehearsing for this, so much needs to come on the spot rather than everyone knowing exactly what to do. It breeds creativity if you're not totally sure about something so you keep thinking about it and then the ideas start to flow. All of the Band were creatively flowing now.

I booked the Lodge Recording Studio for the 24th of May, 2004. Northampton is not the best place for parking, it's a bit of a nightmare to be honest (just ask Dean Rees when you see him,) as indeed most city areas are becoming. Rob offered to drive Karl and I in if we got to his place between Bedford and Northampton. The second week however Rob would not be there so often but it was cool being driven in style in Robs late model Range Rover. Karl and I were the only ones to attend every day. Dean did when he could, parking his van outside and getting a ton of parking tickets. As I sometimes do in another town or city, I parked in the Fire Station around the corner from The Lodge. One night walking back to my car with a guitar slung over my shoulder I noticed the crews standing outside, engaging in the usual banter of firemen....sorry Fire Persons! "You going to shoot us or serenade us?" One of them shouted in my direction. I turned around so they could see the GIBSON logo on the case. "Ahh, serenade us" "You're all too ugly" I shouted back. They did save me a fortune in parking tickets though.

Chapter 15

As I outlined earlier, I prefer to initially lay down guitar tracks, then guide vocals, then build up the rest, piano/Hammond etc and finish off with the vocal proper. I like to have the total feel of a track before I do the lead vocal and I know Melanie feels the same way. I will sing differently once I know where it's going, trouble is everyone feels the same. You will play differently once you get feedback from everyone else but to do everything at once takes a big chunk of input space to the mixing desk and sometimes is just not possible. So with this album we would try and do it half-and-half, some of the tracks were recorded more or less live, the rest layered as outlined.

Dean started on the Monday morning moving in everything that goes with a Hammond. Max and Robert liked the idea that we were using the original sound of the Hammond, they had a smaller Hammond in the studio but Dean likes to play with his own Organ. (Sorry had to put that down at least once!, won't do it again, promise!)

He has two 'Leslie' cabinets, the creation of Don Leslie. These are a unique speaker that spin around in their cabinet and causes a sort of tremolo effect. Many effects try to re-create this but the real 'Leslie' does sound different. You can get samplers that have Hammond sounds but a real Hammond for one thing, has much more power. He can also make it overdrive, almost like a guitar 'Power Chord,' it sounds very progressive when you get it down to tape. (Sorry....digital hard drive.....no....it doesn't sound the same does it!)

With Dean set up on one side of the studio area and Karl's drum kit at the other, it was getting a bit tight for space. The gear could stay all week though so no sweat there.

Once they were all in and happy, they went for a drink, (it was dinnertime) so I stayed and started with the guitar guides. With luck I wouldn't make too many mistakes and could keep some or all of them. We began the guides for 7 tracks. We originally intended doing 3 tracks in Rob Butterfield's home studio but after the first week of recording we all agreed things were starting to sound so good in the Lodge it might be a bit of a drop in standards if we used Rob's semi pro facility. So we quickly made plans to 'Live Record' another 2 tracks, stretched a couple of tracks out and we would have 45 mins.

For me, this is THE 'real' thing about music, to go into a studio and make something no one else has ever heard before, it's new, it's unique and it's yours. No one will have ever heard it before and I still get excited starting a new album and I hope I always will. With luck things can turn out better than you ever anticipated.

We varied putting different things on first, second etc, the songs were taking shape. Rebecca Gibson was due in on the Thursday, we'd need a fair bit on before then. Rebecca was going to do tenor sax and flute. Mel has done a lot of flute on our recordings in the past but her hospital duties have meant she is at her own admission, a bit rusty. She was all for Rebecca doing it. I was starting to beam as the week progressed. Every dinnertime we'd end up in the bar a few doors away, I was going to miss that too when we were finished, even though I don't drink, its a great atmosphere and a bit of 'Male Bonding'!.

Piece by piece the jigsaw came together. On one track I was scheduled to do the lead vocal. 'Time To Move On', was now a Reggae-ish song but my voice didn't seem to fit. I tried it straight and I tried it gravely, neither seemed to work. It was a good song but it needed a different style of vocal.

I persevered, did an acceptable vocal and decided to leave it for a while, see if I or anyone else would come up with any new slants on the track.

Everyone worked exceptionally quickly, we had to, even at the good rate they let us have the place for, it was still racking up a lot of money to be in there. If we could work fast we could do this within the budget planned.

One song I was looking forward to doing was 'As The Lights Go Down' lyric supplied by Isabel. It is a political song and very meaningful. I did the first couple of takes in a gravely-ish voice and was fairly happy but the faces in the control room said different. Isabel came in for the odd day when her teaching duties allowed, she wanted me to sing it cleanly. I got the hump a little, we had a debate about it and I tried it her way. I have to say her way this time, was better.

The track 'Time To Move On' was left, Melanie was due in on the following Monday and would be doing the lead vocals on 3 of the 9 tracks. I was wondering if she fancied having a crack at 'Time To Move On'. "Sure" she replied. She did it smooth, she did it funky and she did it brilliantly. Karl said to me after. "I was kinda hoping she would have a go with that one, its the best song on there now" He had a point, although I still prefer 'Don't Tell Me'

89

Mel has been singing 'Heart Of Shame' live for 3 or more years but I did the original in 1997. This was going to be her finest hour. Everyone who hears 'Heart' thinks its an older Black woman singing, they are astounded my 22 yr old daughter is the voice behind this powerful track.

'You're Alone' is a Blues track, the type I love doing. This was the first time I'd used my Epiphone semi for soloing and I was more than pleased with the sound Max was getting with this and all the guitars. Rebecca came in and worked as quickly as anyone, her flowing sax was just what was needed on 'No One Can Tell You'. I had tried to do the solo but it didn't seem to fit. Dean likewise. When Rebecca did her bit, it fell into place.

*OH FATHER!*

As a lot of you will know, with computer mixing it is possible if you have a bum note in there, to change it for a good one with the computer. Be it a voice, guitar, horn, anything. You just punch it up on the screen, change the offending note and it's perfectly in tune. Now whether you think a lot of today's 'Artists' use this device overly you'll have to decide for yourself, I couldn't possibly comment.

Anyway, in a line on one of the tracks, I went a bit flat on one note. Max said, "Don't worry Ben, I'll just change that one in the mix". Melanie was sitting behind me. "You get back in there father and you do it properly this time!!" I looked at her thinking she was joking.....her face, or more accurately, her 'Spock eyebrow' told a different story!!

I have to admit though when the same thing happened to her, Max again offered to change the offending note to which she replied "No, I'll just sing it properly this time" and she did...That's my girl.

The second week was spent tidying up the odd vocal and bits of guitar etc. Starting to feel a bit sad now because I knew I'd miss this. I also knew I would miss Elsa she is Max's Doberman and the studio mascot. She would sit on our laps, or rest her head on a lap throughout the entire fortnight. I love Dobermans, they are so intelligent. I had one right after Sam died. She was the best behaved and the smartest dog I ever had.

The 2<sup>nd</sup> week ended and we were all pleased with the tracks, I know we all enjoyed it but the next step was looming.

So we had a sleeve, we had the tracks. We had a plugger. Distribution was now the main issue. Well, one of them....there was also the small matter of getting people to buy it!!

Chapter 16.

*DIVVY UP!*

Throughout June I was planning the possible ways of getting the money together, the entire project would cost around £3,000, mine would be the Lions share but Karl and Dean gave a very big chunk. We had worked out all the royalties and every one was happy with the way it panned out. If we as a band, signed a recording contract to a label it would go something like this. For the Band i.e. performing on recordings, approx 10-12%, approximately another 5% for the producer or Executive Producer(s) (those that pay for the studio time). Songwriters get 6.8% of retail, this is set by the P.R.S. & M.C.P.S. of which as stated previously, I am an Associate Member. This song writing royalty has been changing somewhat in recent years because there is no stability in retail prices. The mail order companies sell CDs much cheaper than the retail network so many record labels are trying to work the composers royalty on a 'Trade' price as opposed to the retail as it's usually more stable.

Many labels can and do sign artists for less than the 10% outlined but the governing body sets the composer's royalty. So you sometimes get unequal situations occur, e.g. in the early Beatle contract, I think it's known the Beatles or Brian Epstein, got the deal with Parlophone for 1d (old penny) for every seven inch record sold. As singles were then 1s 11d that worked out to about 4% of retail for the Beatles as Recording artists. However, as the vast majority of the songs were written by Lennon & McCartney, their composer's royalty worked out to more than the artist royalty even taking into consideration the percent N.E.M.s took from Lennon & McCartney for publishing rights. This can get you very bogged down, working out recording royalties is an accountants job and most bands don't go into this properly until they've been ripped off a few times.

*CRISIS!*

We were getting there, although I'd still not got distribution but that would have to wait for a while.

Julia was on holiday with friends in Majorca or Mallorca as the locals write it. She was staying in Palma, she phoned fairly regularly, for Julia at any rate, the holiday was going ok and she was due to fly back on Tuesday 20th July. On the Monday night she and her friends were struck down by stomach upset, probably from a meal eaten the day before. Julia's diabetes has usually meant EVERYTHING effects her much harsher than normally would be the case, a stomach upset even more so than usual.

She was quite ill on the Monday, her friends looked after her and phoned Julia's mother every few hours to keep us fully appraised of the situation. On the Monday night she became worse, falling in and out of coherence. I talked with Sharon quite a few times during the day by phone, going around to her house later that evening to discuss it further. Julia's friends seemed to think she was not so bad now so we left things for now knowing as long as she got to the plane the next day, once she was home we could get her on the mend. During the night she became much worse, the friends called Sharon on her mobile while she was at work as a teacher the following morning, she immediately came home and called me. Julia was very ill now and they had a hard time getting a response from her so we told the girls to call a doctor urgently. This they did, the doctor came quickly and summoned an ambulance which took her to the hospital under Lights and Sirens! Julia was on the edge of diabetic coma, her levels were really wild and she was getting worse by the hour.

The friends had to fly back that night, if they didn't, they would end up stranded with no way of returning home. They were in fits of tears and didn't want to leave Julia, the last day or so had taken its toll on these 2 young girls and they sounded in a bad way. All of us were worried sick about Julia now, we could not contact the hospital, we didn't even know which one she was in. "Right, I'm going out, now!" I said. Sharon agreed, together we booked an emergency flight. (Thank you Britannia Airways!) I started sorting out how to make the journey, it was now mid morning. Melanie was off for the day, I cannot remember why but I was so glad she was. She called me at Sharon's and asked if I wanted anything from the Supermarket, I gave her a list. I had to be at Luton Airport by 5.30 to fly out for 8pm. Luckily, 5 months earlier I had applied for my first passport. The Band had been offered a festival Gig in Macedonia, we never went but I thought it was time to get a passport as many gigs of this nature were starting to come to us. I know this will sound weird to anyone reading but I have not travelled abroad in recent years, never had anyone to go with, so I was a bit daunted to say the least about what I was about to experience....Anyway, I digress.

Melanie drove home with me and helped me pack. She issued orders (in a very nice way) "You'll need some shorts Dad, it'll be very hot and you won't always be in the hospital" She saw my cut down jeans which were getting a bit dog-eared. "Where are some newer jeans Dad?" and she set to work with the scissors on them.

We headed off to the airport, Sean, Benji in the back, Melanie and Sharon. We were all feeling grim, we did not know at this point how Julia was, we'd not heard from anyone for 3-4 hours. I just prayed she was going to be all right. We all sat in the airport lounge, talking about this and that, all of us were quite nervous but being upbeat as much as possible. Mel, (quite a seasoned traveller), began telling me what to expect with my first commercial flight. Soon it was time to go to the boarding lounge, they all gave me a hug. I winked at Melanie, "Don't worry, I'll bring Julia back safe and sound, you see if I don't", there were a few tears around.

Before we had left the house earlier that evening, my old friend Paul Millard came across and chatted. We'd both taken Spanish in our school days. "You'll be surprised how much you remember, it'll start coming back". I was very nervous. I'd never flown by airliner, hadn't been abroad since the New York crossing with one exception, a day trip to France as a boy.

I went through the usual passenger routine, as I made my way up the aircraft steps I could hear some shouting in the distance. I could hear the whole gang as they were shouting and waving me off but now I was on my own. The air stewardess's were great, they knew why I was on the flight as it had all been hastily prepared. I had a door seat next to the window. The trip passed quickly but now I just needed to see my daughter. One of the Spanish-speaking stewardesses wrote out a paragraph on a piece of scrap paper for me to give to a taxi driver at Palma airport. It was now 11.30 local time and dark when we landed, I made my way as fast as I could through the me lee of passengers in and around the airport, grabbed the first taxi driver I could see and showed him the scrap of paper the stewardess had given me on the plane.

Christ knows what it said, I'm guessing something like "My name is Mr Ferrari and I'm here testing out new Formula One drivers, show me how fast you can drive!!" because we were flying down the Motorway in Palma overtaking Police cars with their blue lights flashing!!! I thought they're going to pull us over at any moment but thankfully they didn't. He was touching 110 mph on the journey, around 170 kph.

The 15 min journey ended at the Clinica Jueneda near to the centre of Palma. I went through the reception doors and could see there was just a skeleton staff on now as it was very late. A drunk had just passed me in the entrance doors, his face cut and badly bruised from some incident he had undergone earlier that night, he was English!

I managed to convey to the male nurse on reception who I was and who I was looking for. Julia was, as we'd been told, in the Intensive Care unit. A nurse came out of the lift. "Ah yes, for Julia Markus" her English was passable but she could not give me any answers to my questions about my daughter. At the time I did not know if this was due to her bad English, or was there another reason? We went back into the lift, she pressed Basement level 2! I thought there are no wards on Basement Level 2!! We travelled down, I could feel myself starting to panic and I could feel my blood pressure rising as my face got hotter. "Oh Christ, they're taking me to the morgue! that's all that's down there in the basement!" Was the only reason I could think of for going down to that level. My worries were compounded as the lift doors opened, the décor was all granite walls and ducting, no way was this a ward!!! I began to think they had waited until now to tell me and all I was here to do was to identify a body!!

I followed the nurse in total silence, not wanting to follow but having to. If she had taken me to a row of drawers all that was running through my head was, I would not let her open one, I would stop her. This is not the way it was going to turn out.!! These were the disjointed thoughts now flying around my head but thankfully at the end of the very long roughly decorated corridor..... was the Intensive Care Unit.

We went through the airtight doors and I was informed I had to dress in shoe coverings, cap and gown. I was shaking by now but managed to calm myself, I was taken to Bay 4..... I will never forget the sight before me. Julia was fully prone, about 4 intravenous drips were divided into both arms. An E.C.G. was set up and it was easy to tell she was really out of it. I held her hand, after a minute or two she opened her eyes and feebly acknowledged my presence. "Hey Dad, sorry" was all she said. I gave her a big hug as my eyes watered. She didn't speak any more that night, The nurses would only let me stay for about 15 minutes and then I had to go as it was well outside the normal ICU visiting times.

## Chapter 17

I didn't want to leave the hospital, I somehow felt I was abandoning my little girl but I had to. I don't think I've ever felt so utterly alone before and I hope I never do again. I was now in a foreign country, I had two pieces of luggage with me, it was around 12.30 in the morning and I had no hotel and no reservations. Plus I couldn't speak the language!!! Boy I could so easily panic now!!

Going back up to the ground floor level I returned to the nurse I had originally seen in the reception area, who's English was fairly good and told him my situation. "Ah, you want Hotel Araxa just down in the town, they treat you pretty well from the hospital". He called me a cab which arrived within 10 mins. I got in, the cab driver while very friendly, wouldn't take me to Hotel Araxa. "No, Hotel Husa Zenith much better for you" I tried to argue but I really couldn't be bothered any more, I was just too overwhelmed by it all. "Fine....take me where the fuck you want!!" was all I said.

Hotel Zenith wasn't too bad, 3 star I think, the staff were all very friendly and sympathetic over the coming 3 days. Trouble was, and the taxi driver knew this! It was about 6miles from the hospital, whereas Hotel Araxa was just within walking distance. (I say walking very lightly! as you will later read). The cabby had obviously been touting for business from the hotel. I couldn't be bothered to change hotels for now, I was waiting to see what happened.

The Intensive Care visiting hours were very limited, half an hour 8-8.30 morning, 1.00-2.00 dinner-time and 8-9 PM evening. Julia was looking a bit better as I arrived on the Wed morning. She was talking and knew what was happening around her but she was on constant monitoring. I think the biggest problem at this point was the presence of Ketoacidosis in her system, whatever book you study....this is BAD!

It's a process that can occur with a diabetic when the exchange of carbo-hydrates is not going normally. Keytones will show up in the blood and in the urine, this condition is not treated lightly by medical staff. Although Julia had been diabetic since 9yrs old, if memory serves, she only suffered mild ketoacidosis once and a low percentage at that. Her level was now high! Why or how she got sick was not the hospitals main concern, the overriding problem was to bring down her blood levels of glucose and stop the ketones showing in the blood tests. I came back at each session and she slowly seemed to improve. When I first arrived, Julia's blood glucose level was, in the

Spanish system, 250. UK figures are quite different, in the UK a normal level of glucose is approx 3.5- 6.5. So I knew the 250 was a figure worked out on a different system but what was the conversion formula? On UK system, you're dead by 40. If Julia were high in UK numbers, it would be around 15-20. So I asked many doctors what the dividing number or formula was so I could compare but no one seemed to know. I mistakenly estimated to divide by a factor of 10. (I arrived at this figure because the doctor had said he wanted Julia to be around 120 level. Which would be around 12 UK if the factor of 10 was correct. The 250 level of the previous night would then be approx 25, which was high enough to be causing her illness.)

That night I went back to the hotel, I called Sharon and Melanie after each session and we were all fairly happy about Julia's progression. On the Thursday morning things got MUCH worse. Julia was looking simply awful, she was again getting to a non-conscious level and her blood level sprang to 380 on their system. So I mistakenly thought this was now 38, very high, but what made this situation much worse was the fact she had been on constant surveillance and an insulin drip and STILL her blood refused to normal out! I'd NEVER seen this happen before, I truly thought we were losing our daughter! More drips were hastily put into my daughters arms as nurses and doctors began to run around the bed. The E.C.G. was plugged back in and her heart began beating an abnormal beat as the high levels of sugar and keytones in her system attacked her bodies normal functioning. I didn't want to leave again but I was more or less ordered out of the ICU. I was now in a trauma driven state. I called Sharon while I was still in the hospital reception area, she'd given me her mobile phone, my brick wasn't up to the journey.

I started to break down on the phone. "I think you'd better think about coming out here Sharon, I'm not sure if Julia is going to make it through this. I think we might be losing her!" Just saying that made me worse, I had to cut the call short. On the way back to the hotel in the taxi I didn't know what to do and how to react, I had no one there I could talk to and the hotel room became like a prison.

Sharon called me back herself in floods of tears and we discussed the entire situation at length, I gave her everything that had happened that morning, Sharon too was in a bad state. She would begin the process of arranging her flight out but she would wait for me to call again at dinner-time.

I'm sure many of you reading this have felt at one time or another that feeling when things are really black, we, well I, tend to operate on a sort of automatic level. You try and cut out your inner emotions because it's the only way to cope or go forward with the things you have to do. You become very detached from your inner self. I was now at this stage, operating on a very detached level, I wasn't eating and much more importantly, *I wasn't drinking any water!*

I knew not to drink the tap water, the only establishments I visited in my daily routine, were the hotel and the hospital and I was slowly de-hydrating. Thursday dinner-time visiting session came and I was the first through the doors to the Intensive Care Unit at the Clinica Jueneda, bang on 1 o clock, maybe a bit before. They weren't gong to stop me! Julia had, I'm very glad to say, turned the corner. Her levels were beginning to drop and she looked a little better, she just managed to pick up a hand and wave at me as I bent down to kiss her. She had so many drips and monitors in her now that no matter which way she turned, she just couldn't get comfortable. She was having to stay on her back otherwise she would've pulled everything out. Her heart still however looked an unstable pattern. (Watching my fathers ECG over a long period and watching him die of heart disease, I did have a rough idea what it should look like!)

The main ICU doctor was great, the staff were giving Julia a 'VIP' treatment probably because she was so ill, maybe because they knew how she was feeling being in a foreign land etc. Later on we both thanked them for how they made the time much better than it might have been. The English translator came around, I asked what the formula for the blood levels conversion was. Now the doctor understood the question. "You divided by a factor of 18!" Ah, so the 250 level though bad was around 13-15. The 380 was 21 and NOT 38 as I feared. Even so, 21 while under complete medical surveillance is very bad.

The doctors, now she was over the worst of it, began theorising as to the reason for Julia's crisis. It seems Julia and her friends had had a seafood dinner on the Sunday., if this meal had a bacterial infection in it, (2 of the other girls suffered stomach upset, so it is likely) this could have been the culprit. Bacteria will feed on insulin as insulin is a protein, therefore a food, and a very rich food at that. The bacteria will consume huge amounts of the insulin, in a non diabetic you just keep producing the insulin and weather the infection out and other systems deal with the invasion, sometimes we need help in the form of anti biotic s. But Julia has a finite amount of insulin to deal with this type of situation, which can and in this case DID, become near fatal.

Julia hasn't been the best at looking after her diabetes, she always injects but she has, over the years, been negligent with regard to blood testing. However, I truly do not think she was in anyway the cause of this illness. Who the Hell cared if she was, she was slowly on the mend. She did improve with each visit, up to the point we were now playing cards. (Mel had slipped a pack into my bag before I left, bless her).

We invented a new game based on the old 'Sevens' that two people could play, called it Sietta (I don't know if that's how you spell seven in Spanish?). As I mentioned, I wasn't drinking or eating much. By the Friday I set about to change hotels to the earlier recommended Hotel Araxa. It was a couple of blocks away and I could now walk to the hospital. The new hotel staff were also fantastic, it was a much plusher hotel, air con in every room. Hotel Araxa gave discounts to Hospital referred customers so the price was the same as Zenith.

Friday dinner-time I set out for the mile or so walk to the hospital for the dinner-time visiting session. I was in shorts, I hadn't previously taken note or realised just how hot it was in Mallorca. It was at least a 100 every day, sometimes higher. I was in shorts, a tee-shirt and (thank you Isabel) my Yankees baseball cap. Just like the one Derek Jeter wears!! (I also have a bat JUST like the one Bernie Williams uses!!) Thank God Mel told me to take that. (The cap, not the bat!). It's probably the only hat or cap I would wear, I always hated wearing hats and I said I would never wear another after the 10 years in the Fire Service when I had too.

I had a Holiday makers map to direct me to the hospital but I should've known holidaymaker type maps are not always totally accurate!! Yup, I got lost. It was now around 12.44, the hottest part of the day. The main drag I was following now looked like a dual carriageway that ran near to the hospital but it wasn't. Whether or not I was on the wrong road, or the map was just badly drawn I don't know but I'd been walking briskly for nearly an hour and I saw nothing I could recognise. I was sweating quite a lot, it was hot, it was very hot. I saw no other living thing, let alone people to ask the direction to the hospital, they were all tucked up in their air conditioned rooms, they weren't crazy enough to be walking around Palma in the noon day sun in mid July!

I actually thought I was doing pretty well, I was still walking, had all my faculties, thought to myself..."This is a piece of Piss, don't know what everyone makes a fuss about, I can take this heat!!" but the lack of any real water intake over the past 3 days was at work. I did eventually find the hospital. Later on, after a nurse looked at the map I was being directed by said "You were about 7 kilometres away from the hospital, IN THE WRONG DIRECTION!!

As I went through the reception, feeling proud for not having collapsed up until this point, I started to see dots before my eyes, things began to look a little black and white. I was starting to feel a trifle light headed as I made my way into the ICU. Julia looked at me with sort of an askew glance. "Are you ok Dad? I think you'd better sit down!!" "I think you're right Julia" was my feeble reply but I didn't wait for a chair, I just slumped to the floor!!! Nurses and doctors began running from all directions, this time towards me. They put me on another bed next to Julia, hooked me up to the E.C.G. and blood pressure meter and told me to relax. "It's ok I kept saying". So now we, or rather I, was the story of the day in the Intensive Care Unit, father comes to see daughter, ends up in next bed!! Every time a nurse came in to see Julia, she started chuckling!

Julia was also chuckling away...."You wait till I tell everyone!!" "I was just a bit de-hydrated, that's all" I replied but I don't think anyone heard me. My vitals returned fairly quickly to normal but I did start drinking water by the litre from that point on though.

*TAKE ME BACK HOME*

Julia was deemed well enough to be transferred to the normal ward on the Saturday. She was handed over to a different doctor on the main ward and she didn't like him a whole lot, he was ok but I could see what she meant. In the UK, diabetes is dealt with on a much more laid back basis, patients are allowed more freedom with diet and can alter their insulin accordingly. He was right out of the Spanish Inquisition. His manner was brusque, his ideas antiquated and he told Julia. - "Before you leave I want you to be on a very strict diet. You will eat what I say and when I say" I know this is an exaggeration but that's the way he came across. He was used to a regimented way of treating his patients and he was to be obeyed. Now this doesn't go down that well with Julia. "He's looking for a Slap!!" she said after he had left the room. "He's going to get one if he talks to me that way again" she continued. "Oh, great Julia, they'll never let you go then....You want to get home don't you?" yea she answered in one of her many funny voices. Julia had not seen the other members of her family for nearly a fortnight now.

The normal ward was very different from the ICU, it looked more like a hotel, if a sparsely decorated one. One bed rooms made up the long corridor of the 3$^{rd}$ floor where she now was, everything was new but somehow very bare and plain. However I could now stay all day with my daughter. We carried on playing cards and we did have a view of the sea from the window so things were looking up. Julia was allowed to walk around, she still had one drip in though so a wheeled contraption had to follow her around. The television was....well....imagine Star Trek in Spanish! It really doesn't do anything for the programme!

I had fetched her baggage from the hotel she and her friends had stayed at and bought them back to my room at the 'Araxa'. She wanted some of her luggage, in particular her make up in a bid to start feeling normal again. So now the job at hand was to get the hospital to let Julia go home, she was aching to be back in Bedfordshire and so was I.

Now I was starting to relax a bit, Julia was getting better and it would just be a matter of time now. I began to wonder around Palma on my frequent trips to the hospital and started to take notice of my location. It was very different from England but good different, I started to think along the lines of how I would love to visit more places in the world, I wonder if I'll ever get the chance?

## Chapter 18

The weekend passed slowly in the hospital ward, we chatted a lot, we watched television and we played many card games. We actually grew a bit closer again. You know what it's like with your teenagers, they start doing their own things, you're doing your things too and you just start to drift apart. I just wish it hadn't taken such a BIG crisis to start this little 're-bonding bit but the worst was behind Julia. We watched the Formula 1....Guess who won?? and just to make things worse, we were watching on a German Television Channel. Boy can those announcers say 'Schumacher' a lot of times within the space of a minute!

The Gothic looking doctor called in a few times over the weekend, I told Julia to bite her tongue...she did. On the Tuesday the doctor thought she might be well enough to go home. Where Julia was concerned, there was no 'might' about it. I told her, "Don't worry, if they won't let you go, we'll get a couple of moustaches, a couple of big Spanish sombrero's and sneak out" Sort of a joke but also sort of close to the mark.

We had to satisfy the hospital (and by that I mean the Conquistador!) Julia was well enough to go home and more importantly, fit enough to fly. So we both lied a bit. Obviously she couldn't fake blood glucose levels but she was being very upbeat whenever the medical staff were in the room. I knew however she was still weak, watching her walk across the room blatantly showed that but you have to choose which would make her worse, staying there a few more days where she would get more and more depressed or helping her fake how she really felt, so we faked it.

Tuesday morning we were sitting in the Consultants waiting room while he prepared some documents to say she was discharged. He gave them to her, shook our hands and wished us well, probably not a bad sort really, just used to a different atmosphere with regard to dealing with patients.

We arrived back at my hotel Julia said "Christ Dad, this is better than my hotel was!" Her hotel had reminded me of a Butlin's type place whereas the Araxa was very stylish. We sat around the pool for the rest of the day and ordered a meal at lunch-time. Julia was eating now, a little bit at first but eating. She was checking her levels, I wondered how long that would last once we got back to England but I have to say she has changed her attitude a bit on this front.

Now the airlines (who had been aware of the problems from the beginning) wanted EVERYTHING signed in triplicate, cross-signed etc etc. They could not take chances for insurance purposes on Julia's state of health. There was a flight, again with Britannia to leave around 7.30 that night, it was now 5 o clock and the insurance company who were dealing with everything STILL had not finalised things. Julia was anxious, I was worried because Julia was anxious and things started to feel like we may not be going home. I phoned the Insurance agents about 4 times in the space of an hour but written hospital consent had still not arrived at the airport desk. I said on the phone, "we have no hotel now because we've booked out, they have no spaces left, if we DON'T get a flight I have a young girl just out of hospital with nowhere to sleep and you don't know if we can go?? We have to leave for the airport now if we're going to catch that flight!"

The insurance company told us to make our way to the airport and they would try and sort things out, which Bless them they did but it was touch and go right up until boarding time.

The two of us sat around the airport lounge, had a bite to eat and waited for the flight home. I know I was fussing a bit, I'd had reason to this week. Julia got a little fed up of the treatment - "Dad, I'm ok, please lay off a bit" OK I replied but it's just so hard to let them go and be in charge of their own lives, we all have to do it though!

The flight back was uneventful, Julia listened to music, I watched the TV. With about an hour to go before landing I said to Julia, "They (meaning the family) will go pretty nuts when we get through the arrival gate you know". "Yea I know" but all she could think of was the fact she was approaching home.

I was right, they did go nuts!. Everyone was there, Ric accompanied Mel, Sharon rushed for Julia and they stayed in an embrace for close on 3-4 mins. Melanie was in there hugging too, Benji had tears in his eyes and so did Sean. (Although he tried to hide it.) The emotions were indescribable. I paused for a minute, just a minute and thought how completely black this could've all been. After she finished hugging her sibling, Melanie embraced me like the fears of the week were just starting to let go.

"Thanks Dad" was all she said. "I told you I'd bring her home ok" I replied but there had been more than one time in the last 8 days when I seriously had doubts about that but it all ended very very happily.

God I could get used to that laid back way of life on a Spanish Island or possibly the Spanish mainland, maybe one day, when I've accomplished what I think I can accomplish.

Dean, Karl and Isabel had been in touch the entire time. Karl sent a text just after he'd heard I'd collapsed in the hospital that did make me laugh. I took a couple of days out and recharged myself. I knew it would take some time getting over this whole episode but the way it all ended made that a Helluva lot easier.

So, it was time to get the manufacture sorted for 'Time To Move On'. Back to the lovely Karen who's S.R.T. is not only still going but going strong. Many companies in this line of work have gone to the wall but S.R.T. is doing very well due to the fact they have an exceptional name in quality for CD production. You can get some very bad jobs with CD manufacturing, some don't complete the post production mastering properly, sometimes not at all, instead they clone whatever master you take in. (That is to say no EQ-ing is performed on the original recordings.)

I contacted local designers 'Fresh Ammo' to have a go at designing the sleeve artwork John Deery had taken over the place for a week while Fresh Ammo's owner Chris Williamson was on holiday. I met with John, told him what I wanted, handed over everything I had, photos, acknowledgements, prayed I had everything right and sat back and waited for John to call to say the artwork was finished.

He was very quick, just one day when he called me in to have a look, the final piece to the jigsaw was there. The artwork was everything I hoped it might be and a bit more besides. I could tell John was pleased too.

The artwork I find is the biggest area for complaint with regard to the printers, they do apparently have the ability to mess a lot of original artwork up. The colours can come out wrong with the finished product and silly errors can be made with the wording etc. Whichever firm Karen used was spot on. The colour resolution on the front sleeve was if anything, better than the computer masters had been. I thought the illustration originally was a shade too purple but when the finished albums were completed, they had been made a bit more blue and turquoise. Very Appealing!!

The night I picked up the consignment from the St Ives offices in Cambridgeshire just happened to be the night of the worst thunder storm for the year. As I approached the offices in Edison Way I could see a flooded area and some lorry drivers were standing by it. I really didn't think it was going to be that deep but the water started coming over the bonnet of my ageing Honda Accord as I drove through the flood. The lights were now under water, it was washing up over the side windows. I just had to keep going, had I stopped, the engine would have cut out as the water level was way over the exhaust pipe, if anything I put my foot down harder to create a wave in the water hoping the speed would keep the engine dry. I thought when I stopped the engine, this won't start again because I'd not done any maintenance on the old heap for....well.....Ever!!

As I pulled into S.R.T.'s yard I could see Karen at the door. "I was going to phone and say the road at the bottom was under water" she said. " You don't say" I replied. "It's ok" I continued. "I'm here now" She made a cup of coffee and we waited and chatted until her delivery driver arrived with the CD's.

Opening up a box from the newly delivered crates, I held the new album, it was worth the wait. The whole year, everything because now we had an album to show the world. Karl called for about the third time that evening. "Are they done? have you got them?" I replied positive. "Can we meet so I can get my lot?" "Not tonight if that's alight Karl, I'm knackered!" He said "OK" but his demeanour said the opposite. I then remembered how I felt especially when I was 28 about making something new like this, the excitement and the need to do and see everything at once! (Christ, I'm in my forties and still feel the same way more or less!!!)

"OK Karl, usual place let me go home and change first, I'm soaked". "See you there at 9" he replied.

The storm did not let up all evening, it was an horrendous trip back. When I pulled into the 'Griffin' car park in Toddington Beds the entire village was blacked out. None of the pumps were working in the pub and the electric had been out since seven that night. I sat in the candlelit pub drinking bottled tomato juice with a long haired brunette!!..... Who's beard was longer than mine! "You tell anyone that you and I have sat here having a drink by candlelight Karl, I'll kill you!" "Why" came the reply "Don't you think I'm good enough for you or something?"

I handed over a CD. "That's absolutely BLOODY FAAANTASTIC" was Karl's only reply, it did look good. The CD case back was my favourite piece of artwork but the picture disc also looked an expensive 'quality' item.

Karl took his boxes and took an equal amount for Dean after we had a few drinks, then we both went home.

*LET DOWN YET AGAIN*

Throughout the entire process of making 'Time To Move On' I had been in touch with a few distributors. One who shall remain nameless (but you know who you bloody well are!!!) said they would take the album, I have quite a few e-mails where they were discussing deals etc, methods of promoting but now it was finished....they had simply changed their minds. That's ok I thought, people in this industry have done this to me quite a few times, it wasn't out of the blue, there are enough companies around.

Richard Lim runs Avid Distribution, he had been with the old 'P.R.T. company', so we have some background. I've seen him a few times over the years and he agreed to a meeting to discuss 'Time To Move On'. My ageing Honda, the one I went jets king with a few days previously, was looking a bit tired.

I know it shouldn't matter how things look but we all know that it does, I'd just not changed cars for a few years now. The Honda had still done under 100,000 miles, still ran like a dream and never attracted attention despite having several £thousand worth of guitar hidden in its boot when I parked it in London streets. No one cared about it and no one looked at it but now however, its tattiness was a negative thing.

The meeting with Richard Lim went well, we discussed the plans for promotion, the live work, then, when the meeting was finished and Richard Lim was going to mull it over for a few days, he offered to walk me to my car. "No, please Mr Lim, it's really not necessary!" "I insist said the small Oriental man".

"Is this your car?" He said very nicely but I thought Ohh Crap!!

People think that if you're doing ok, you have to have a good car. If I was down on luck and I could not afford a decent car... how the Hell could I bring out a record!! It just meant my comfortable old Honda would have to go!!

I got a newer Peugeot, a smart 405. Quite a top of the range model. It's older than most people's I know but still a 90's model. The first distribution company I approached and managed to get an appointment with AFTER acquiring the newer car, gave me a deal. As I said before, it shouldn't matter....but it does!

I had made approaches to 4 or 5 distributors by now. S. Golds in E17 were most likely to be the distributor for 'Time To Move On'. Peter Connell while hard to get hold of at first, was very efficient and also very keen to have a go at selling our album. You could tell he organised things well and he offered a Consignment deal whereby we gave them a specific number of CD's and when they sell those, they order more and pay for the first batch, so forth and so on. This would probably be better for us at this time as we would not have to sign a sole distribution contract, we could take our time on that one. Carl Palmer of Jetstar Records and Distribution, always a Gent, had called me a number of times and expressed an interest to take the new album for sole distribution. He is a very well known Reggae dealer but I know he wants to branch into other areas of music, 'Rock' being one of them. In the end however, we went with the S Golds contract.

# CHAPTER 19

## POWER OF THE PRESS!

'Blues Matters' the well known Blues bi-monthly magazine is owned by Alan Pearce, Alan Pearce gets things done. He's been editing the magazine for many years now, wants to see Blues a much bigger item than it has been for a number of years in the UK and has started a record label to go with the magazine.

Sending out the usual copies to ALL the music magazines and newspapers, Alan was one of the first to get back to me. "I really like 'Time To Move On', it hasn't been off the CD player since it came into the office!"

He continued and told me he would REALLY like to sign the whole Band to his record label. This could very well be the thing we need, the Band are constantly discussing the pro's and con's of this deal. (We are meeting tomorrow night in the usual place again to see what we're going to do but I hope we get some talking done before they all get pissed again!!)

We are still pushing the album and the single to radio stations. As of Nov 2004, Isabel has managed to get the single on 10 I.L.R. stations. She has had 2- 3 days at the BBC in London, going around Radio Two, Radio One and back to Radio Two plus many many phone calls to both seats of power.

Anyone in this line of work will know Clare in the reception of Radio One. She is a certified 'Darling'! She virtually organises the building, has done since Melanie was a 7 yr old and used to accompany me. Now Melanie's voice is the voice on the recordings we take around !

Clare arranged for Isabel to see the Radio One producers, it was by all accounts very different from Radio Two. The pluggers stand around the halls, dressed, well, a bit like Kevin and Perry. Radio One was not the audience we aimed at with the single but you have to give them a few here and there otherwise you'll never know. Both of us were not really surprised when the bulk of the Radio One staff said it was 'Too mature a sound' but as always they gave us their time and were interested in what we were trying to do.

Handling the Retail promotion myself, we have managed to get Virgin Mega Retail to buy the

album nationally, a big coup for an own label! Thanks this time to Ryan Berry of Virgin. Charles Holmes of HMV is also interested and wants to be kept informed of all movement and publicity we get....

As 2005 began the winter months dragged on, I attended Sean Markus's first gig with his own band 'YELLOW BELLY' Not knowing what to expect my eldest son was nervous as he should be. They were playing with 2 other bands at the Barton Football Ground Social club. It was a Sunday afternoon/evening and the place was starting to get fairly full. Karl knew of the 'first gig' and to use his term "Aint gonna miss that one Ben" Karl, his wife Carolyne and their two children were in attendance as was Sean's sisters, brother and mother.

Is that really my little boy standing on the stage with a Strat around his neck?? The boy who just a little while ago I was winding as he lay over my shoulder? Christ they grow up quick. The band consisted of Sean's class mates.
The kicked off the first number which began with a soloing lick from Sean, not only did he NOT fluff anything, I was quite amazed at the overall sound. Most of us were there for support, parents and families coming to cheer offspring but they were sounding pretty good. Karl was standing next to me on a chair at the back of the hall. "Ben, I thought they were going to be the usual crappy teen band......they're not, they're doing ok!" with genuine surprise in his voice. "I know" I replied...."Maybe we've got the 2nd guitar?"

MEL AND RICK.

On April 16th 2005 Melanie Rose Markus married Richard George in Barton le Clay Church. She looked utterly beautiful as she readied herself for the big day in her life. Melanie had wanted Julia to accompany she and I in the wedding car, there were a few protests from family members who said "That's not the way its done really Melanie" but Melanie insisted, so did Julia and I fully agreed. Those two had been so close over the years, played together, cried together, grew up together and it seemed fitting they should ride in the limo together.

The day was truly fantastic. Melanie had wanted a smooth jazz band to play at the after wedding ceremony (I really think she thought Sean and I would've hi jacked the musicians as they entered the Marston Moretaine venue for the after celebrations had they been a guitar based band......thinking about it......she was probably right!) but it was just the right atmosphere. I watched as my

little girl danced first with her new husband, then her little brother Benjamin and Julia dance with Sean and all four of them looked as happy as I'd seen them at any time in my life. It's a satisfying memory I shall carry for eternity.


SEAN GEOFFREY aka 'BOB'

Over the coming months I talked with Sean at length if he wanted to slum it with his Dad's Blues Band. He was more than enthusiastic for the chance. "It won't be the heavy stuff you like or are playing in your own band" I told him. "That's ok Dad" So in March 2005 Sean began rehearsing with the album line up and the alternative line up I use when Karl and Dean are busy with the HUMBLE PIE commitments, this includes, VICKY COWLES on Sax and keyboards, my son in law RICK GEORGE on bass and now Sean Markus. The rehearsals went well and before long we were ready for gigging with my eldest son.


Sean's first appearance with 'MARKUS' just happened to be a live 'Unplugged' session for BBC RADIO. To be recorded in Northampton, it would go out on many of the local stations as they link up at weekends and evenings.


The BBC producer called me on a Wednesday morning. "Can you come this Saturday and do 3 or 4 acoustic tracks?" "Sure" was the not so confident reply I gave. When things like this drop in your lap you have to say yes and work out how to do it later. It wouldn't be too much of a change really. Just do the usual electric stuff with acoustic guitars, Karl could use the snare drum and bass drum for a solid rhythm and Dean agreed to bring his electric piano.


Melanie readily agreed to take part so the 6 of us were scheduled for the Saturday dinnertime slot on June 25th 2005. The producer told me to be there for 1.30 to 2.00 pm. Northampton is not the best car friendly town but we were doing ok, it was 1.15 and I was in the town area. Dean called me on my mobile. "WHERE THE HELL ARE YOU LOT?" his voice was higher than usual. "We've got to start playing at 1.35!" No point arguing, I just drove as fast as I could. We pulled up in the BBC car park at 1.30 dead, grabbed the acoustic guitars, Mel and Rick were behind me. We virtually ran into the studio, sat down and started playing, no time to tune up, no time to run over things, just play. 'Heart of Shame' from TIME TO MOVE ON was the first track. I'd not heard Melanie singing for a while. She just stepped up to the microphone and let rip. Her voice was powerful, smooth and fantastic. I glanced over at my two children, Sean had a smile on his face, he was thoroughly enjoying the event. Mel was concentrating on singing but even through the concentration there was a look of satisfaction on her face as she stood there, eyes closed belting out a song she's sung a hundred times before.

We came to the end of the song and BBC DJ Richard Jordan just said "Wow Melanie.....how do you sing like that?" Still on air Melanie replied "I just open my mouth and it all comes out" Simple but true.

We did the remaining 3 tracks and completed a 10 min interview about what we were doing, where we were playing and the new album etc. As we all walked out of the building with guitars and equipment in hand. I could feel a very satisfying aura all around us. Sean and Mel gave each other a hug, Karl and Dean all slapped Sean on the back, hugs all around really. We climbed into our vehicles and went down to the nearest pub and mulled over the performance.

This is what its all about for me. It's not about the money, yea I know we all need it to survive but THAT day summed it all up in my mind. The world only seems to make sense to me when I have a guitar around my neck. I am just so very grateful I found my niche in life.

A few weeks after this I wanted to take some more photos for possible sleeves. Sean and little Ben came too as it was still school holiday time. Sean's getting quite good with the camera, judging the overall size and content quite good. The track to be made a single would be the title track from the album – 'TIME TO MOVE ON'.....I thought....railway tracks, you know....moving on...

Sean and I went down the line at the old Stewartby level crossing in Mid Beds. Sean said more than once "What if a train comes Dad!!" "Just take the photo Sean......this is Art!"

With the modern wonders of developing digital photos in less time than it takes a Norwegian to buy Ski boots we had a good photo! I said to Sean, "some people like to use an alias for photos, you know, an 'Arty' name. Do you want to use one?" He thought for a minute or two then just said "Bob!" "Bob" I replied? "Bob" he said. Okaaaay!

October 2005 and I was toying with the idea of doing some re-recording on one of the album tracks. It's so hard to single out a recording in the early stages and get a feel for what can be improved or made bigger. I'd had nearly a years feedback and had some idea which songs people liked and preferred.

Everyone seemed to prefer this or that but EVERYONE liked the title track 'TIME TO MOVE ON'. Melanie had originally sung the lead vocal on this, I thought I would have a go and put mine on. Nothing at all wrong with Mel's vocals. She has in the past year, been compared to the likes of; Joss Stone, Cher and many other well known singers. I think she sounds like Melanie Markus but we all like to compare to people from our backgrounds.

I approached her with my ideas and she was enthusiastic as always. I wanted her to do some 'Big' backing vocal lines, make it a big production. The Lodge was booked for October 6th, Sean would have his first go at recording onto a track destined for production. He seemed quite cool as usual about the whole thing. He knew the track, I just said "Come up with a rhythm line that is different from what's there Sean"

10 am on the mentioned morning I was knocking on the door to the Lodge, in the middle of Northampton town centre. Max opened up………"You've cut all your hair off Max!!" I was used to seeing him with long hair, he now sported a number 3, damn near as short as mine (number 1 now, shaving took so damn long to do every morning, although I still start to feel like a Hippy if I let it grow further than a number 3).

We walked into the control room and set down all the guitars. I had ALL of them with me. So many times I've taken one or two, then as things start moving have thought to myself "Wish I'd bought the 12 string, or one of the others"

Melanie was due in about dinnertime having to work a half shift in the morning at the hospital. "Right Sean, do you want to go first?" I asked. "Not really" came the reply. "Ok" I continued, "I'll put a lead riff throughout the track"

I picked up the Epiphone semi and peeled the case off, began the tune up procedure. So many times I've seen or heard people do a guitar take without tuning properly, then afterwards complaining to themselves the guitar was out of tune. For live you can get away with a quick tune but in the studio, set aside 15 mins and get it spot on. It's worth it believe me.

Max downloaded the original multi recording from the DVD and was nodding as he remembered the original session 12 months earlier and what mixing/effects etc he'd originally used.

I did the solo take twice, kept both copies and Max said he'd use bits of one and bits of the other. "Fine by me" I replied.

Then I re-did the vocal where I was going to sing it. Slightly different melody than Melanie's and I phrase things differently.

Then it was Sean's go. As he tuned up his SG he began to look nervous. He sat by Max and ran through the recording, playing along. Max was nodding appreciatively as my eldest son began his recording career. I stood well back to give him room and not to show I was overseeing but I wanted to hear this moment.

After his first 'real' take his brow showed a bead of sweat. "Christ I didn't realise I'd feel this nervous!" he said. "Not like playing in your bedroom is it" I quipped to my young son. He'd done a take which was to be honest ok, Max said "You can do better than that Sean, have another crack at it" By the 2$^{nd}$ take he had it in the bag. Max was just a little unsure about a few lines in the 2$^{nd}$ verse and got him to do a 'Drop in' and Sean was finished.

Vicky Cowles, the other half of the brass section, was coming in to do a much bigger brass piece. We'd worked out the line a few weeks earlier. I tend to like brass with Rock and Blues to be a unison piece as opposed to getting the horns to harmonise with each other. Straight octave unisons tend for me, to sound more 'Blues' you put too many harmonies in and it starts to sound a fusion thing. Vicky had her baritone, tenor and alto saxes with her. She began the riff with the tenor, spot on first time, double tracked it, then triple tracked it. All the same notes, then repeat process with the baritone. Again with the alto, so we had a 3 octave unison riff going and with about 10 tracks, was sounding very big. While limbering up with the alto sax, Vicky began jamming to the track.

113

"Put an alto line over the last two choruses" I told her through the desk microphone. She did and the track was sounding like a huge production, just what I wanted.

Melanie by now had called me twice and was a little lost. Lodge is a bit hard to find.................well it's not really but Mel's place finding is a bit suspect!  I can remember thinking when she first passed her driving test she would go off in the car and that would be the last I'd see of her as she
failed to find her way home again but she's been driving quite a few years now and chose to make a long distance motorway trip within 10 days of passing her test.

Melanie called me for the third time, I was outside the studio on the verge of jumping out in front of a red Corsa and flag my little girl down. Trouble is my eyes are not quite as good as they used to be and more than once I nearly jumped out in front of the wrong car!!
She called to say she was in another car park in the town, I sent Sean off to find her. They met up and duly arrived at the Lodge.

The recordings were all done to the usual very high standard and actually became one of my favourite tracks of my own material.

Chapter 20

Chapter 19 was written in 2006, Christ how time simply passes away, it's now January 2012, we did the TIME TO MOVE ON revamp. I managed to get an Arts Council grant after a lot of backing and forthing with Arts Council forms and applications. FURTHER ON DOWN THE ROAD came out on CD for 2008 although quite a few blips and problems with distributors meant it was not truly available until 2009. I felt it was probably the best album
I'd done to that point and it's sales while not earth shattering, were encouraging.

I and a varying line up of musicians did some gigs and more radio shows, in particular the 'acoustic' sound was becoming very popular with the radio shows and presenters, so this was emphasised and a new album planned throughout 2011 to take this folk rock concept further.

GRETA.

However, sometime in 2009 I had been chatting to a friend and telling her about a remarkable woman I had known growing up. My friend began crying as I relayed the story.

Gertie was well known throughout Pulloxhill, the villagers having been told she and her husband were Austrian and had moved there sometime as the Second World War had ended. Gertie was an intelligent, beautiful woman and she kind of adopted me when I was that awkward young American kid trying to fit in with English life in
a rural village.

It was now around 1994, Melanie and I had been visiting my parents grave in the Pulloxhill Churchyard when I noticed Gertie's husband had died and his stone was in place. I felt sad and knew Gertie must be devastated, I said to Melanie "Lets go see and old friend" she readily agreed. We walked the few hundred yards to Gertie's cottage overlooking the green, I was not even sure she'd still live there but it was a starting point, (she'd probably not remember me if she did live there).

My daughter and I climbed the steps to her garden area, Gertie was crouching in the garden, when she saw me she nearly screamed "BENJI!"

She rushed up and gave me the biggest hug I'd had for along time, right away seeing the family resemblance in my daughters face. "So, this is one of your children?" I nodded with a grin, "Yes and she has a sister and a brother. She made us all drinks, wanted to know Melanie's interests, chatted at length with her and then it was my turn. With the various albums I'd made over the years I had received some publicity in the local papers and a few articles with a couple of National newspapers.

She knew about them all and even kept a few clippings, I was astounded to be honest but we talked at length and I just said at the end of the visit. "I saw your husbands grave in the Churchyard, I'm very sorry Greta". She didn't say too much as she became emotional but she just said, come back soon. "I will" I promised.

I did return to see her as promised and was quite astonished to learn not only were her and her husband not Austrian, they were German, Gertie had been a Concentration camp prisoner and her husband had been a Camp Guard!

When I re-told this story to Viv, she simply said "That's the most heart rendering story I have ever heard". I stopped and thought....by God it is isn't it.

So I undertook to write a story inspired by and loosely based on Gertie's life. Titled GRETA the manuscript took 18 months to complete. When finished I began contacting Literary Agents, publishers etc but while the interest seemed genuine and even enthusiastic with some, but by December 2011 it had still not made it into print.

August 2011 I had been working out as I always did in my bedroom, a pain slowly began in my chest, then grew to the point I quickly became unable to move, managed to get to the bed and tried my damnedest to relax. I had the strongest feeling I was undergoing a heart attack!

The pain was getting out of control and the panic deep in my soul made it all worse. I closed my eyes and willed myself to relax...it was bloody neigh on impossible but the pain eased a

116

little. I made my way downstairs and took one aspirin. My Fire Service medical training came to mind and I remembered taking one aspirin can save a life.

Within 3 minutes of swallowing the pill the pain subsided considerably to the point I could reach the phone and call for assistance. I originally called my GP, the receptionist asking if it was Urgent?...Damn Right was the reply. She told me to come in right away but the GP himself called within 10 mins and told me the best action was to call 999 as they had the clot busting drugs should they be needed.

The Para-Medic team were at my house within 15 minutes and I was now in the kitchen with a mobile ECG hooked up to my chest. The rhythm seemed ok (I more or less knew what a good beat should look like having spent hours watching my fathers ECG as he slowly died). The head para medic said "Doesn't look too bad but I think we should take you in to A&E for a full check out".

I was loaded into the ambulance unit and taken the short drive to Bedford South Wing's Emergency Dept. Melanie was not on duty today, she had been a very proud mother some months ago and now worked part time. Amelia was my first grand daughter and the spitting image of her mother!

The medical staff began running tests and taking blood...gallons of blood! (well it felt like that). By midnight on the 12th of August the Cardiac Registrar covering me thought I could be released and dealt with as an out patient. I was happy with this, all pain had subsided and I was feeling ok. He did state quite firmly, if anything happens again, call right away and get yourself into the hospital. I promised I would and got a lift home with Ric.

The following day I just relaxed and contemplated what would come next dealing with this as an outpatient, then the Sunday I just made a quick trip to the local supermarket and started to experience slight pains in the chest area along with the weird feeling down my left arm.

It was getting worse, this actually scared me more than the original incident, one episode can be put down to a variety of one time events but this was more. I made my way home, thought about it for a while and realised they would take me back as an in patient, so I was going to enjoy the summer's day and deal with that Monday!

117

I got the Yamaha out and made my way to Paul's house, I didn't labour the heart situation but I did give Paul a hug before leaving "What the hell is that for!!" (Paul was never the demonstrative type!) Had a lovely dinner with Melanie, Ric and Amelia.

Amelia Rose George was my first grand child. Melanie went through a lot of pain and had a very tough birth...but the outcome was well worth it as she took to motherhood so very very easily and loved every minute. Amelia and I became instant friends and NOT because to use Melanie's term "You let her get away with everything!"...ok....maybe I do a little...now and then....

I then made my way to Sharon's and had tea with her and Benji. Monday morning I rang the Cardiac Care Unit and was told to come in right away prepared for a stay. 30 mins later I was admitted through Accident & Emergency.

The cardiac registrar who discharged me Friday night said " Why did you wait till now if you had the pains Sunday?" "I wanted to have a normal Sunday" My only reply. He began organising tests etc and I was put back on the ECG permanently as the world went about it's business. Everything once again seemed normal but an angiogram was set up for first thing Tuesday morning. This was in fact Melanie's team lead by Dr Cooper, Mel had wanted to assist but the surgeon said "I'll be a bag of nerves if you're in there with me" so she waited outside.

The procedure was planned to be approx 40 mins, a camera on a flexible tube  is inserted into the groin area, or if they believe it to be a fact finding mission as this was, via the main artery in the arm/wrist.  20 mins into the procedure Dr Cooper just said "Oh Christ!"...I was awake but sedated at this point, "Oh Christ?....what does Oh Christ mean!?" He just said calmly "I'm going to put you out now" and that was the last I heard...

Two and a half hours later I woke up, the camera along with the injected dye had found a 95% collapse of the LAD (big artery in or near the heart....medical people love to abbreviate everything!), a stent had to be inserted right away and so it was.

Melanie had hung around and was on and off the ward as I came around, Dr Cooper came onto the ward about 7 that night and said "You were very lucky, you were a very short time

off a cardiac arrest, no one was expecting the collapse as your ECG and blood-works were fine".
Seems I dodged a bullet!

My recovery was pretty good and they let me home on the Thursday, Friday morning
there was a very evident sign of internal bleeding, I called the hospital and was told to get back
in...less than 8 hours home and returning yet again.  Rashmi next door was great and
gave me a near 'lights and sirens' trip to Bedford South Wing Hospital. This time I was
placed on a surgical ward as the heart all seemed fine.

I had been given a list of drugs to take to assist the heart in it's recovery, thin the blood too
so the stent could bed in. One of these was called Clopidogrel and is classed as a 'super drug' due to
the fact it seems to repair heart tissue. I had not suffered an MI (myocardial infarction) so the heart
muscle, tissue etc was all classed as good but the Clopidogrel would ensure
any missed defects would be dealt with as well as it's main job of making the blood less sticky, once
again so the stent could bed in easier.

This time I was kept 5 days, the bleeding stopped and all seemed ok, so I was let home on the 23rd
August 2011. Two days later...back on the bike, I felt a little woozy but that's the best
cure I know for such an ailment, the weather was really nice now too.

After a couple of weeks of taking it steady I started putting together another acoustic line up
to do some more radio stations. I had made some tweaks to the FURTHER track HOLD ON which
was a reggae tinged version of the old Sam & Dave classic. Melanie shared lead
vocals, we had a very big horn sound, a ton of backing vocals and I managed to do get Sean to do a
guitar duet with me, the track was a peach!

Through a musician site called Band mix I managed to meet up with Jon Digweed (bass) his wife
Sandy (percussion) Tini Dunleavy and even Alan Mickleborough from the old days of Terry White's
came on board. We worked on vocal harmonies and the 'unplugged' line up was
sounding really good.  We were invited on to BBC Cambridge with the lovely Sue Marchant who
had given me and Elise Darches a spot Easter 2010 on her show. After 7 at night a lot of the BBC
local stations link up, so Sue's show goes out to a very large chunk of England, Beds, Herts, Bucks,

Northampton, Suffolk, Norfolk, Essex all get the Cambridge show, so it's damn near as good as National Radio Two, some might say even better!

Sue invited us all on her show October 25th for live music and chat, it went down very well but all accounts and this line up seemed destined to get some good coverage and attention. More radio shows with Trev French on Wolverhampton City Radio, Biggles FM, The Eye, several London stations were all planned and booked. The Wolverhampton station was

a fair distance and I booked a lot of appearances for that week finishing with a Bedfordshire station on Saturday 5th of November. On the Sunday I started experiencing a lot of pain in the lower stomach area, this gradually got worse to the point I was literally climbing the walls by Sunday evening. Tini had been in touch during the day and realised I was in trouble. It was just a stomach ache...no need for hospital! But she insisted I get someone to take me in.

Sharon thankfully offered to take me in, Benji was now old enough to look after himself and she turned up within 15 minutes of the phone call. The A&E team at Bedford once again took me in within minutes of turning up to the reception, seeing I was by now in great pain and could not stand up straight. I didn't even realise but I was also in urine retention which as some of you will know, is bad. Over a litre had now backed up and urgent action was needed in the form of a catheter, I can't say it was an easy procedure and I'll leave it at that!

Seems I was still bleeding internally too so a lot of tests were ordered, seigmoidoscopy, colonoscopy, blood tests, the list went on. One blood test showed a PSA level while not exceptionally high, it was high enough to warrant further attention. A biopsy was scheduled for the prostate on the 13th of December. Prostate cancer is classed as the least dangerous cancer, at least that's what all the doctors were telling me. So even if it come back positive, it was very treatable and not worth much concern.

Meanwhile around the end of November a German publishing company, Just Fiction Edition had seen references to my story GRETA. Evelyn Davis of the company had made a search and found The Markus band website along with a contact e mail and wrote to me asking if she could see the GRETA manuscript. Due to the health issues I really was not checking the band e mails so it sat unread in my in box until the middle of December.

I found the e mail and it really did brighten the day and whole month. I quickly wrote to Miss Davis explaining the situation why I had not been checking e mails, she wrote back within a day asking if she could see the entire manuscript, I sent it back immediately.

Seven days later she wrote back offering me a publishing contract for GRETA, the terms were good and I accepted. By mid January 2012 the e book was on sale and the paperback was due in a couple of weeks.

On the 5th of January the biopsy result was given to me in South Wing hospital. Seemed I had a very rare and aggressive form of cancer in the prostate. SCC for those of you who know. The doctor and his assistant said a number of times how sorry they were, I was not sure what was really happening at this point, the second they said rare and aggressive, the questions coming out of my mouth and forming in my brain were far outweighing any answers they were furnishing me with. A lot more scans were going to be needed.

Melanie bless her was there for me yet again, as she's always been. She was now a senior radiographer, "Tell the cancer unit and the radiography dept you can attend any cancellation appointment and you can get into the hospital within 20 minutes" was her sombre advice. Seems people cancel these appointments all the time, an MRI scan can take 3-4 hours, if someone cancels, the machine can stand idle for that time.

My first allocated appointment had been the 16th January 2012 but it was now January 12th and all six scans were completed late on Thursday evening on the 12th, the last CT scan was arranged with less than 2 hours, "Could I get in right away and take the preparation, hang around for 2 hours?" Damn right was my only reply.

It was now the 20th of January and the medical team had all the information, scans, bone scans X rays etc. I had an appointment to see the main cancer specialist, Dr Sharma in Bedford South Wing, a lovely man and very caring doctor. Melanie offered to come with me despite being 5 months pregnant, I accepted.

We sat as Dr Sharma outlined the bottom line. The cancer had spread from the prostate to the lymph nodes, it was a very aggressive cancer but they were going to try to treat it as a cancer specialist at Addenbrookes hospital Cambridge thought he had a treatment plan to fit this rare attack of cancer cells. (Dr Sharma said this was a differential cancer, Melanie got the gist of it all and she later explained to me as we left the doctors office).

The treatment however was going to be tough. Seven weeks of radiotherapy EVERY day!...hormone injections which were to start that day and then it was very likely Chemotherapy would be needed at the end of the 7 week period. The doctor went on to say at first I won't feel too different but by the 3$^{rd}$ or 4$^{th}$ week I was going to start feeling bad....really crap as Melanie put it later. But for now...they were going to treat it! To be honest, that morning getting myself ready for what be the most important meeting with a medical expert I'd ever have, I couldn't help thinking, it had spread too far (the specialist nurse had told me on the phone on the 18$^{th}$ Jan the cancer had spread outside the capsule, I knew this was bad).

I told Melanie we'd get everyone around and I'd buy dinner that night as a celebration, I could see the look in my children's faces, especially Benji, sort of a "my dad won't be beaten by cancer" look....

Once again it was a memorable night at my eldest daughter's house with her husband and little girl with most of the family in attendance. I drove home around 9 as the day had taken it's toll. Then sat in an empty house and the enormity of my new situation started to hit me.
I've got SEVEN weeks of intense radiotherapy EVERYDAY! At the end of the seven weeks it was likely I had to undergo Chemotherapy too!...hormone injections...etc etc...driving to Cambridge every day for 7 weeks! I was less than 6 months over the heart surgery...how the hell can I cope with this too!!!???

## Chapter 21 Epilogue

I'd thought long and hard about how I was going to finish this tale, do I wait and see the outcome of the cancer treatment? Do I write about how crap I felt at any given time??....No...

I am going to leave it all up to your decision and judgement. You put a happy or sad ending on this and end the story yourselves. At this moment I'm still pretty positive and that might change over the coming weeks and months and I don't want to write that down, especially if you happen to be in a similar position, my experience might taint yours and I don't want that. So that's it, I hope it goes on from here and there's going to be a NEW JERSEY EXILE PART II!....or maybe RETURN OF NEW JERSEY EXILE?...Kind of catchy I thought.

If you really want to know how things turn out...you can always go to the MARKUS BAND website at www.themarkusband.com

The main site won't carry up to date news, but the facebook page of which there's a link, will do. (but don't peek before reading the whole story!).

I would like to dedicate this book to anyone who has been diagnosed with cancer. Anyone who's heard the words from a medical professional "I'm so sorry but I'm afraid it's cancer", will understand why.

## DISCOGRAPHY

THE FOLLOWING DETAILS ARE COMPLETE AS OF 2012.

ALBUMS;

*'NOCTURN GATE'.    Artist - BEN MARKUS.*
*Released June 1983. Cat No; 83 CUS 1844.*
*12 inch vinyl album. Label; Ooze Records. Distribution; P.R.T. Mitcham, London.*

*All songs written by Ben Markus unless otherwise stated.*

*Tracks;*
*S1, 1, SHOT IN THE DARK. (MARKUS/CROSS). 2, ACHING TO SEE. 3,SECOND TIME AROUND.*
*4,WHEN YOU'RE GONE. 5,NOCTURN GATE.*
*S2, 1,YOU LOSE. 2, LIFE IS CRUEL. 3, TOLD BEFORE. 4, PROMISE TO SHOW. 5, RECANT.*
*Produced by Ben Markus, Nigel Pegrum, Joe Bull and Steve Woodward.*
*Recorded at; Pace Studios, Milton Keynes, Bucks and Spaceward Recording Studios, Ely, Cambridgeshire.*

*Musicians; Ben Markus, guitar, vocals, backing vocals. Steve Woodward, bass, guitar, backing vocals. Alan Valance, drums. Nigel Pegrum, drums. Vince Cross, keyboard/piano, backing vocals. Mark Williamson, bass, backing vocals. vocal arrangements.*

*'JUST A SHAGGY DOG STORY'.   Artist - 'THE BEN MARKUS BAND'*
*Released Feb 1990. Cat no; CITCD 202*
*Album, CD and cassette.  Label, Citation Records. Distribution, Supertrack/EMI and TERRY BLOOD DISTRIBUTION Newcastle.*

*All songs written by Ben Markus unless otherwise stated.*
*Tracks;*
*1, ANGELENE. 2, THE FEELING'S RIGHT. 3, WEARING THIN. 4, ALL I KNOW. 5, NO ONE CAN TELL.*
*6, WHITE ROOM (Bruce/Brown). 7, PROMISE TO SHOW.*
*8, CAN'T GO BACK. 9, YOU'LL NEVER KNOW. (B.B. King).*

*Produced by Ben Markus and Nigel Pegrum.*

*Recorded at; Pace Recording Studios (Later to become 'LOGICOM' Willen, Milton Keynes, Bucks.*

*Musicians; Ben Markus, guitar, bass, vocals, backing vocals. Vince Cross, Keyboard/piano. Mark*

*Williamson, backing vocals. Steve Woodward, bass. Nigel Pegrum, drums. Julie Costello, backing vocals.*

*Alison Sumner, backing vocals. Rick Taylor, trombone. Gordon Marshall, trumpet. Peter Webber, additional*

*piano. Melanie Harrold aka JOANNA CARLIN lead vocals on 'ALL I KNOW'*


*'RABBLE WITHOUT A CAUSE' Artist - THE BEN MARKUS BAND.*
*Released Dec 1996. Cat No; SPRAYCD 307.*
*CD Album.   Label; MAKING WAVES. Distribution; CM DISTRIBUTION YORKS.*


*All songs written by Ben Markus unless otherwise stated.*

*Tracks;*

*1, YOU LOSE. 2, HEART OF SHAME. 3, LIFE IS CRUEL. 4, SO FAR AWAY. 5, OVER YOU. 6, ALL I*
*KNOW. 7, LOST YOU TOO (Quintentton). 8, YOU'LL NEVER KNOW (B.B. King). 9, PROMISE TO SHOW.*
*10, IS IT RIGHT. 11, WEARING THIN. 12, OUR LOVE (AIN'T MADE IN HEAVEN). 13, CARY GRANT*
*EYES.*
*14, ANGELENE. 15. TOLD BEFORE.*

*Produced by Rupert Cook and Ben Markus.*
*Recorded at; LOST BOYS STUDIOS Cranfield, Bedfordshire and Pace Milton Keynes, Bucks.*
*Musicians; Ben Markus, guitar, vocals, backing vocals. Melanie Markus, flute,  vocals, backing vocals. Ian*
*Paul, trombone. Jay Alibone, tenor sax. Simon Porte, drums. Peter Lubbock, bass. Martin Hart, piano.*
*Alison Sumner, backing vocals. Julie Costello, backing vocals. Rupert Cook, bass, guitar. Julian Simmonds,*
*keyboards. Steve Foggin, drums, trumpet on 'Our Love'.  Nigel Mills, piano on 'Our Love'.*


*'MAGIC GARDEN' Artist - MARKUS.*
*Released Dec 1997. Cat No; SPRAY CD 309*
*CD album.   Label; MAKING WAVES. Distribution; C.M. Distribution, Yorkshire.*


*All songs by Ben Markus unless otherwise stated.*

*Tracks;*

*1, RUNNING (Blunt). 2, ALL I KNOW. 3, ONE MORE TIME. 4, YOU'RE MINE (Blunt). 5, I DON'T NEED*
*YOU (Markus/Blunt). 6, HERE WITH YOU (M. Markus/B. Markus). 7, TIRED, (Blunt). 8, CAN'T GO*
*BACK. 9, CRY ME A RIVER (Arthur Hamilton). 10, DON'T YOU LIE. 11, MAGIC GARDEN*
*(Markus/Blunt).*
*12, HOLD ME (Blunt).*

*Produced by; Ben Markus, Stavia Blunt and Max Read.*
*Recorded at THE LODGE RECORDING STUDIOS, Northampton.*
*Musicians; Ben Markus, guitar, bass, vocals, backing vocals. Stavia Blunt, piano, keyboards, vocals, backing*
*vocals. Melanie Markus, Flute, vocals, backing vocals.*
*Simon Porte, drums. John Morrey, bass. Max Read, bass, keyboards.*

*'NEW JERSEY EXILE' Artist – BEN MARKUS.*
*Released May 2001. Cat No; BJM01 501.*
*CD album. Label; BLUE JUICE MUSIC. Distribution, BLUE JUICE RECORDS, Bedfordshire.*

*All songs by Ben Markus unless otherwise stated.*

*Tracks;*

*1, OVER NOW. 2, PROMISE TO SHOW. 3, ONE MORE TIME. 4, I DON'T NEED YOU (Markus/Blunt). 5,*
*LIFE IS CRUEL. 6, HERE WITH YOU (M. Markus/B. Markus). 7, YOU'LL NEVER KNOW (B.B. King). 8,*
*DON'T YOU LIE. 9, WHITE ROOM (Bruce/Brown). 10, CAN'T GO BACK. 11, TOLD BEFORE.*

*(As this was an amalgamation of the earlier albums, musicians and recording studios were as previously*
*stated with the exception of;*
*Recording studios used. CREAM ROOM, Ware Hertfordshire. MILLENIUM STUDIOS, Southend.*

*'TIME TO MOVE ON' Artist - MARKUS.*
*Released Sept 27th 2004. Cat no; PLG 33566.*
*CD album. Label; CITATION MUSIC. Distribution; S. GOLDS, LONDON E17.*

*All songs written by Ben Markus unless otherwise stated.*

*Tracks;*

*1, GOT TO GET AROUND YOU (B. Markus/I. Fulcher). 2, TIME TO MOVE ON.*

*3, NO ONE CAN TELL (B. Markus/D. Rees/K. Randall). 4, HEART OF SHAME.*

*5, AS THE LIGHT'S GO DOWN (B. Markus/I. Fulcher). 6, DON'T TELL ME (B. Markus/M. Markus). 7,*

*OUT IN THE COLD (B. Markus/I. Fulcher). 8, YOU'RE ALONE. 9, BEING HERE (B. Markus/I. Fulcher).*

*Produced by; Ben Markus, Dean Rees, Karl Randall and Max Read.*

*Recorded at; THE LODGE STUDIOS, NORTHAMPTON.*

*Musicians; Ben Markus, guitar, vocals, backing vocals. Melanie Markus, vocals, backing vocals. Dean Rees, Hammond Organ, piano, backing vocals. Karl Randall, drums. Rob Butterfield, bass. Rebecca Gibson, flute, tenor sax, backing vocals.*

*'FURTHER ON DOWN THE ROAD' Artist – The Markus Band*

*Released; Sept 2009. Cat No; PLG 33568. All songs by Ben Markus unless otherwise stated.*

*Tracks;*

*1, FURTHER ON DOWN THE ROAD. 2, HOLD ON (by Isaac Hayes & Dave Porter)*

*3, ALL I KNOW. 4, IF I DID'NT KNOW BETTER. 5, GOT TO GET AROUND YOU (unplugged version) (B Markus I Fulcher). 6, TIME TO MOVE ON. 7, HEART OF SHAME. 8, LIFE IS CRUEL. 9, CITY. 10, DON'T TELL ME (B Markus & M Markus)*

*11, AS THE LIGHTS GO DOWN (funk version) (B Markus & I Fulcher).*

*12, OVER NOW. (Abbey Road Mix).*

*Produced by Ben Markus & Max Read. Recorded at; The Lodge Northampton, OVER NOW recorded at Abbey Road St John's Wood London.*

*Musicians; Ben Markus – guitar, vocals, backing vocals. Melanie Markus – vocals, backing vocals. Sean Markus – guitar, backing vocals. Karl Randall – drums. Dean Rees – Hammond, piano, backing vocals. Rob Butterfield – bass. Ric George – keyboards, backing vocals. Rebecca Gibson – Saxes, flute, backing vocals. Viki Cowles – sax.*

SINGLES

*'LIFE IS CRUEL/WHEN YOU'RE GONE' Artist – WOODMARK*

*Release date; Feb 1983.     Cat no;  OZOO 333.*

*7 inch vinyl single.    Label; OOZE RECORDS. Distribution; OOZE RECORDS.*

*Double A single. Produced by Ben Markus, Joe Bull & Steve Woodward.*

*Recorded at; SPACEWARD STUDIOS CAMBRIDGE.*

*'SEE ME CRY'      Artist  -  BEN MARKUS.*

*Release date; April 1984. Cat no; 0ZO 600. 'SEE ME CRY/PROMISE TO SHOW'*

*7 inch vinyl single. Label; Ooze Records. Distribution; P.R.T. RECORDS, LONDON.*

*Produced by Mark Williamson and Ben Markus.*

*Recorded at; PACE RECORDING STUDIOS, Milton Keynes. Bucks.*


*'WHITE ROOM' Artist  -  BEN MARKUS.*

*Release date; Feb 1989. Cat No; CIT 101. 'WHITE ROOM/CAN'T GO BACK.*

*7 inch vinyl single. Label; CITATION RECORDS. Distribution; SUPERTRACK/EMI*

*Produced by Ben Markus and Nigel Pegrum.*

*Recorded at; PACE RECORDING STUDIOS, Milton Keynes, Bucks.*


*'ALL I KNOW'   Artist  -  GAS-TANK.*

*Release date; Oct 1989. Cat No; CIT 102. 'ALL I KNOW/WEARING THIN'*

*7 inch vinyl single. Label; CITATION RECORDS, Distribution; SUPERTRACK/EMI.*

*Produced by; Ben Markus and Nigel Pegrum.*

*Recorded at; PACE RECORDING STUDIOS, Milton Keynes. Bucks.*


*'ANGELENE'  Artist   -   THE BEN MARKUS BAND.*

*Release date;  Feb 1990. CAT NO;  CIT 103.     'ANGELENE/ANGELENE (instr)*

*7 inch vinyl single. Label; CITATION RECORDS, Distribution; SUPERTRACK/EMI.*

*Produced by; Ben Markus and Nigel Pegrum.*

*Recorded at; PACE RECORDING STUDIOS, Milton Keynes Bucks.*


*'HERE WITH YOU' Artist  -  THE MARKUS BAND.*

*Release date; Feb 2002. CAT NO; BJM02 503. 'HERE WITH YOU/DON'T YOU LIE'*

*CD single. Label; BLUE JUICE MUSIC. Distribution; BLUE JUICE MUSIC.*

*Produced by; Ben Markus and Stavia Blunt.*

*Recorded at; THE LODGE RECORDING STUDIOS, Northampton.*

*'TOLD BEFORE' 20$^{th}$ Aniv EP.  Artist  -  THE MARKUS BAND.*

Release date; May 2003.  CAT NO; PI-33564. 'TOLD BEFORE/YOU LOSE/ALL I KNOW/LIFE IS CRUEL.

*CD EP (extended play) Label; CITATION MUSIC.*
*Produced by, Ben Markus, Rupert Cook, Nigel Pegrum and Joe Bull*
*(tracks dating from 1983-2003.)*
*Recorded at; LOST BOYS STUDIOS, Beds. PACE STUDIOS, Milton Keynes.*
*SPACEWARD STUDIOS, Cambridge.*


*'TIME TO MOVE ON' Artist  -  MARKUS*
*Release date; 25$^{th}$ October, 2004.  CAT NO; PLG 33567.  'TIME TO MOVE ON/NO ONE CAN TELL'*
*DOUBLE 'A' CD single. Label; CITATION MUSIC. Distribution; S. GOLDS, London.*
*Produced by; Ben Markus/Karl Randall/Dean Rees.*
*Recorded at; THE LODGE RECORDING STUDIOS, Northampton.*


*'AS THE LIGHTS GO DOWN' Artist  -  MARKUS*
Release date; Due for release March 2005. CAT NO (as yet to be allocated)

*'DON'T TELL ME/AS THE LIGHTS GO DOWN'*
*DOUBLE 'A' CD single.  Label; CITATION MUSIC (as of time of writing) Distribution; S. GOLDS (as of time of writing).*
*Produced by; Ben Markus/Karl Randall/Dean Rees.*
*Recorded at; THE LODGE RECORDING STUDIOS, Northampton.*


*TIME TO MOVE ON (2006 version)    Artist – MARKUS.*
*Release date; March 6$^{th}$ 2006. Cat No; PLG 33567*
*Distribution; S. Golds London.*
*Recorded at; THE LODGE RECORDING STUDIOS, Northampton.*


*HOLD ON      Artist – The Markus band*
*Release date; 7$^{th}$ November 2011.  Cat No; PLS 33569.*
*Distribution; Amazon UK.*
*Recorded at THE LODGE RECORDING STUDIO, Northampton.*

*Finally I am going to list some people who just through being there, made life much nicer than it otherwise might have been.*

**Melanie Rose George 'né Markus. Julia Emily Markus. Sean Geoffrey Markus**
**Benjamin Lee Markus. Amelia Rose George. Ellie-Rose Markus (second grand daughter and Julia's first lovely girl)**

*Sharon Rose Markus. (we always remained friends and she helped a lot during the dark time at the end of 2011 and early 2012). Ric George. Geoffrey Millard. Paul Millard, (my real brothers). Yvonne Millard.*

**Fire Service**; *Jack 'the Captain' Jackson. Mick Parsons. Mark Frost. Kevin Parker. Pony Moore. Tony Willison. Cliff Dowling. Les Williams. Dick Alder. Bob Ryan. John McTaggart. Rex Burr. Bernard Brown. Pat Wheeler. Dolly Gray . Larry Nixon. Bob Onley. Vic Northwood. Tony Holloway. Tony Durkin. Dick Noah. Pat Sherry. 'Roastie'. Ron Michelmore. Paul Brown. Dick Beaton. Eddie Hedley.*

**Music**; *Karl & Carolyn Randall. Dean & Kelly Rees. Nigel Pegrum. Mark Williamson. Vince Cross. Alan Mickleborough. Rob & Tracey Butterfield. Tini Dunleavy. Rebecca Gibson. Max Read. Robert John Godfrey. John Morrey. Simon Porte. Steve Foggin. Stavia Blunt. Lisa Rocco. Jay Alibone. Melanie Harrold. Steve Woodward. Ray Jenks. John Morton. John Gill. The Bryster. Sue Marchant. Vicky Cowles. Nick Webb. The lovely Karen Kenny 'né Richardson. Bernard at Infinitely. Peter Lubbock. Lorna Reay. . Alison Sumner. Julie Costello. Rick Taylor. Gordon Marshall. Andy Price-Watts. Ruth & Dave Bulmer. Krys O Brien. John Gill. Rebecca Royce. Ian Paul. Sandra Hooper. Jon & Sandy Digweed. Karen Jenkinson.*

**Friends**; *Phoebe Perides. Isabel Fulcher. Debbee Winegar . Mary Adams. Rashmi & Nila Patel. Xesca Dudell . Jo Gentle. Linda Jeffries. Jacqueline Gane. Janet Cohen. Vivienne Sturgis. Pip. Anna Pukas. Penny Askew. Michelle Ward. Tas. Val Gabidon. Cora Tano. Heather Muir-Sage. Tom Brewer. Barb 'D'. John & Sylvia Cook. Dee Amrouni. Margaret Henry. Ann Jones. Marilyn Williams. John Nixon. Roy Shearwood. Stephen 'Ding' Bell. Tom & Jean Aspin. Mark Anker. Pete Vass. Dr Yvonne Webb. Dr H.K Sharma. The entire Radiography Dept at Bedford South Wing hospital. Lorraine Sparrow. Roger Judd. Rachel & Alison Blewitt. Anna Chance. Sonia Taylor. Graham Watkinson. Chris 'the man' Cole. (and brother Stan). Ricky Stringer. Ina Griffiths. John Parker. Bob Parker. Cathy Parker. Gertie. Maggie. Hayley O Keefe. Caroline Byass. Mick Scholey. Ray & Lena Dennis. Wendy Foley.*

Zeitfracht Medien GmbH
Ferdinand-Jühlke-Straße 7
99095 Erfurt, Deutschland
produktsicherheit@kolibri360.de

Druck:
CPI Druckdienstleistungen GmbH
im Auftrag der
Zeitfracht Medien GmbH
Ein Unternehmen der Zeitfracht - Gruppe
Ferdinand-Jühlke-Str. 7
99095 Erfurt